Safed Musli:
A White Gold

GONDI. MANJUNATHA
SANJAY KUMAR TYAGI
K. SRINIVASAN
Depaartment of Agronomy
Tamil Nadu Agricultural University
Coimbatore

ab
Agrobios (India)

Published by:

AGROBIOS (INDIA)

Behind Nasrani Cinema

Chopasani Road, Jodhpur 342003

Phone: +91-291-2643993, Fax: 642319

E. Mail: agrobios@sify.com, www.agrobiosindia.com

Agrobios (India)

First Published, 2004

Impression, 2008

ISBN ... 0

Price: ... 25.00

9 788177 542233

Rs. 850.00 / US$ .00

Published by:
AGROBIOS (INDIA)

Published by: Dr. Updesh Purohit for Agrobios (India)

Lasertypeset at: Shriya Computers and Printers, Jodhpur

Cover Design by: Reena

Printed at: Bharat Printers (Press), Jodhpur

Preface

Indian herbal industry is at blooming stage, however cultivation of medicinal plants is not so easy. It is a challenging task because less is known about their seed biology. Many efforts have not been made to search elite specimens and their propagation. Current cultivation practices of medicinal plants are unsatisfactory and involved destructive harvesting. There is a need for a scientific approach for propagation of medicinal plants and to collect relevant information regarding agro technology, genuine planting material, economics of field cultivation, high yielding varieties etc.

Scientific cropping of industrially important medicinal plant is an integrated approach with agricultural and forestry with optimum land and water resources utilization. In India, various medicinal plants are cultivated and domesticated, therefore, international trade is looking to procure medicinal plant materials from India for the production of pharmaceutical, neutraceutical and cosmeticeutical preparations. India is also making efforts for cultivation, collection, characterization, planned hybridization programs for the improvement of plant species and conservation of medicinal plants, restoring their genetic resources for commercial cultivation.

Indian farmers are facing various problems in cultivation of medicinal plants because of lack of agro-technology, high fees for packages developed by various organizations, lack of planting material, lack of appropriate standards, poor quality control regimes, inadequate research and development efforts, lack of exact market information, dominance of traders and non-existence of the local markets for medicinal plants are deterring the farmers. Knowledge of post-harvest processing technology of plants for the extraction of chemicals and preparations of active formulations is still needed. For this purpose one has to take help of research organizations, private institutes, farmers, NGOs and public sector institutes etc. for better technical know-now of cultivation and post-harvest techniques of medicinal plants.

Since herbs are produced mainly for the export market, the quality of these herbs can be maintained as per the international requirements. This can be achieved through adoption of good agricultural practices and organic farming.

At present, there is considerable gap between demand and supply of medicinal plants. Such an alarming situation forces systematic research efforts for development of proper agro-technology, multiplication of planting material and commercial cultivation of these plants. Thus before taking up the medicinal plant cultivation, farmers should bear in mind the above requirements and constraints. Linking of farming with market in medicinal plant will take time. Therefore farmers should ensure sell of their produce before cultivation. So, with such a plan we can progress and prosper in the field of medicinal plants and achieve an enviable position to lead the world in the trade of medicinal plants.

The purpose of the present book is to give overall information about general cultivation practices, processing and market demand of Safed musli.

Date: 8th June 2004 | GONDI. MANJUNATHA
Place: TNAU, Coimbatore | SANJAY KUMAR TYAGI
K. SRINIVASAN

Contents

Introduction

India is endowed with rich bio-diversity. Medicinal plants occupy a prominent place in country's flora. In India it is reported that over 8,000 plants are having medicinal value out of 17,000 flowering plants, owing to this India is considered as the "botanical garden of the world and treasure house of the bio-diversity". According to World Health Organization (WHO), herbal medicines serve in the healthcare of about 80% of the world population. It also shows that the goal of health for all cannot be achieved without herbal medicines. The demand of plant based therapeutics is increasing world wide due to growing awareness about side effects and complications of chemicals and synthetic medicines, cosmetics, and health supplements. Uses of herbal products have gained importance both in the eastern and western wards. The size of international market of medicinal plant is over US $ 60 billion per annum and India share is merely 0.2 per cent. China accounts for 40 per cent of world trade. This is inspite of the fact that India's resource endowment in medicinal plants is richer than China.

Medicinal plants as a group encompasses a huge number of plant species that are used in Homeopathy and various Indian systems of medicines such as folk medicine, Ayurveda, Siddha and Unani. About 4500 species are used in different folk medicines, 1700 in Ayurveda, 1000 in Siddha, 700 Unani and 500 in Homeopathy. Millions of rural people all over the world use medicinal plants as self-help cure against a number of common diseases. The annual consumption of medicinal plants in the

Folklore systems in India is estimated to be Rs.1000 crores, with invariably locally available species

Planning commission of Government of India in June 1998 has established a task force to study the export market. The task force suggested to fix up the target of medicinal plant export to the tune of Rs. 3000 crores by 2005 and Rs. 10,000 crores by 2010. This is the proper time for India to make relentless efforts to take substantial cultivation and share in current herbal market. Global market data says there is an expanding opportunity in the herbal sector. Market growth rate of 15% per annum in India and 7% globally provides immense opportunity in the sector. Considering inherent strength of India like suitable agro-climatic conditions and vast biodiversity, Indian farmers can easily harness the benefit of this growing market. The controlled collection and sale of large quantities of plant materials from the forest leads to destruction of many forest plants. Local communities, traditional medicinal herbalists and herbal medicine vendors popularly collect roots, bark and whole shrubs. This is a serious problem.

Approximately 627 medicinal plants in trade and only 70 are in cultivation, remaining 557 old species are found only in wild state. Thus the major supply is by the wild harvesting from natural habitats causing fast depletion of natural reserves. India is considered as one of the richest biodiversity zone, which is going to lose due to unscientific exploitation of forest resources especially the medicinal plants. Thus the prime need is given for commercial cultivation of these crops. Currently, Indian farmers have been looking for some better alternative to diversify from traditional agriculture due to gradual reduction in profitability, owing to decline in productivity, increased incidence of disease and pest attack in traditional crops. Contingent upon their hardy nature and high returns, nowadays medicinal plant cultivation is a better option. Cultivation of medicinal plants, especially high value medicinal plants is creating new dimension in the field of agriculture.

The medicinal plant industry puts together the various facts of this multi-disciplinary industry and its global interest. The need for developing countries to acquire technologies and techniques for programmed cultivation of medicinal plants is a current issue. Various aspects of medicinal plant cultivation includes old philosophies, modern impact of traditional medicines and methods of assessing the spontaneous flora for industrial utilization, climatic variations, biological assessment, formulation, process technologies, phytochemical research and information sources.

Recently WHO studies indicate that over 30 per cent of the world's plant species have at one time or another been used for medicinal purposes. Nearly 2,50,000 higher plant species are on the earth, more than 80,000 are having medicinal value. The products relating to about 20,000 higher plant species are being markcted world over. About 120 chemical compounds of plant origin have been developed into modern pharmaccuticals.

Almost 90 per cent of the raw drug material is produced in Asia, Africa, and Latin America and the rest 10 per cent in Europe and USA. India is one of the richest countries in the world with regard to genetic resources of medicinal plants besides China. It approximately occupies 11 per cent of the total known world flora, though its total land mass occupies only two per cent of the globe. Of India's total turn over of Rs.2, 300 crores of Ayurvedic and herbal products, major OTC products contribute around Rs 1,200 crores, Ayurvedic ethical formulations constitute around Rs 650 crores and Ayurvedic classical formulations constitute remaining Rs 450 crores.

The sale of these traditional healers in the countries of European Union was around $ 6 billion in 1991 and is believed to crossover $ 20 billion in 2001. In India the herbal drug market is less than 10 per cent of the European Countries and less than three per cent of the world markets. Nowadays herbal medicines find market as neutraceuticals, which are nutritional or medically enhanced foods with high health benefits. The current market for these neutraceuticals is estimated at about $ 250 billion in the developed countries, which may increase many folds in due course.

The export potential of raw medicinal plants and pharmaceutical products is steadily increasing from Rs.27.18 crores in 1987–88 to Rs.446.30 crores in 1999–2000. Simultaneously, import of the materials is also increased from Rs.13.68 crores in 1987–88 to Rs.60.74 crores in 1993–94 (Table 1). This implies that demand for the medicinal plants for pharmaceutical industries and also for export is still increasing in our country.

Table 1: Trends in Exports and Imports of Medicinal plant drugs in India

Year	Exports (Rs crores)	Imports (Rs. crores)
1987 – 88	27.18	13.98
1988 – 89	39.49	19.70
1989 – 90	70.80	22.65
1990 – 91	69.07	27.08
1991 – 92	129.17	46.54
1992 – 93	127.75	67.76
1993 – 94	167.81	-
1999 –2000	446.30	-

Distribution of Medicinal Plants

Macro analysis of the distribution of medicinal plants show that they are distributed across diverse habitats and landscape elements. Around 70% of India's medicinal plants are found in tropical areas mostly in the various forest types spread across the western and eastern ghats, the Vindhyas, Chotta Nagpur plateau, Aravalis and Himalayas. Although less than 30% of the medicinal plants are found in the temperate and alpine areas and higher altitudes they include species of high medicinal value. Macro studies show that a larger percentage of the known medicinal plant occurs in the dry and moist deciduous vegetation as compared to the evergreen or temperature habitats.

Analysis of habitats of medicinal plants indicates that they are distributed across various habitats, one third are trees, equal proportion of shrubs and the remaining one-third herbs, grasses and climbers. A very small proportion of the medicinal plants are lower plants like lichens, ferns algae, etc. Majority of .the medicinal plants are higher flowering plants.

Trees	:	33%
Shrubs	:	20%
Herbs	:	32%
Climber	:	12%
Others	:	3%

Of the 386 families and 2200 genera in which medicinal plants are recorded, the families Asteraceae (419), Euphorbiacae (214),

Laminaceae (214), Fabaceae (214), Rubiaceae (208), Poaceae (168), Acanthaceae (141), Rosaceae (129) and Apiaceae (118) share the larger proportion of medicinal plant species.

About 95% of medicinal plant raw materials used by the industries are collected from the wild. Over 70% of the plant collections involve destructive harvesting because of the use of parts like roots, bark, wood, stem and the whole plant in case of herbs. This poses a definite threat to the genetic stocks and to the diversity of medicinal plants if biodiversity is not sustainably used.

Whole plant	:	16%
Rhizomes	:	4%
Roots	:	29%
Leaves	:	6%
Flowers	:	5%
Fruits	:	10%
Seeds	:	7%
Stem	:	6%
Wood	:	3%
Bark	:	14%

SAFED MUSLI

Bed Preparation

Manuring

Planting Material

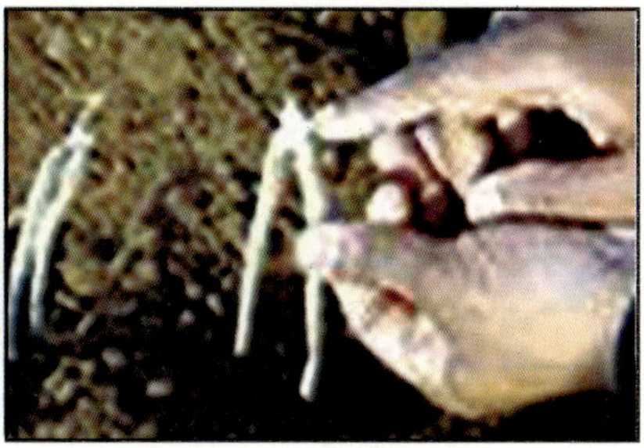

Selection of Tuber

Tubers of Different Size

Seed Treatment

A WHITE GOLD

With Courtesy Patidar Musli Farm, Jotpur (M.P.) Ph:07294-267251, 267351

SAFED MUSLI

Sowing in Flat Bed

Sowing on Ridges

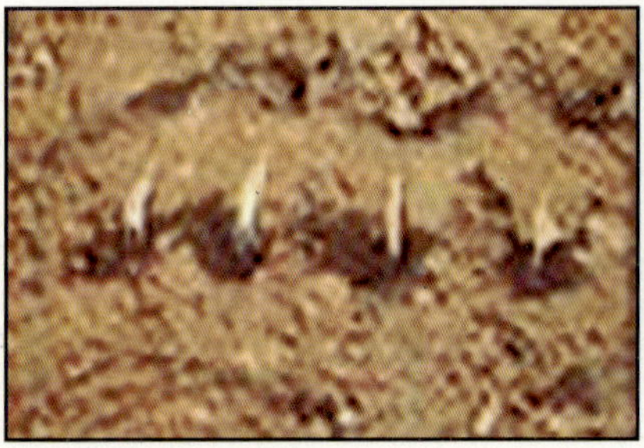

Spacing

Seed Emergence

15 Days After Sowing

Seedling Stage

A WHITE GOLD

With Courtesy Patidar Musli Farm, Jotpur (M.P.) Ph:07294-267251, 267351

SAFED MUSLI

Fertilizer Injuction

45 Day After Sowing

60 Days After Sowing

Furrow Irrigation

Healthy Crop

Flowering Stage

A WHITE GOLD

With Courtesy Patidar Musli Farm, Jotpur (M.P.) Ph:07294-267251, 267351

SAFED MUSLI

Sprinkler Irrigation

Drip Irrigation

Plant Protection

Inter Cropping

Matured Plant

Immature Tubers

A WHITE GOLD

With Courtesy Patidar Musli Farm, Jotpur (M.P.) Ph:07294-267251, 267351

SAFED MUSLI

Post Leaf Fall

Irrigation Before Harvesting

Digging of Tubers

Tuber in Soil at Harvest

Cleaning of Tubers

Bunch of Tubers

A WHITE GOLD

With Courtesy Patidar Musli Farm, Jotpur (M.P.) Ph:07294-267251, 267351

SAFED MUSLI

Storage in Rack

Storage in Trey

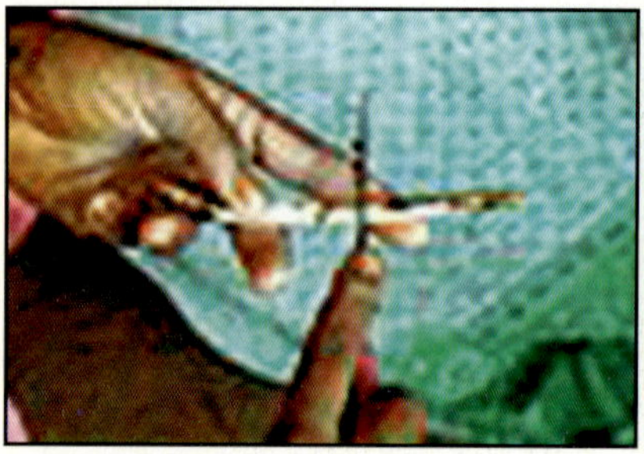

Peeling of Tuber

Peeled Tubers

Drying in Trey

Dried Musli Tubers

A WHITE GOLD

With Courtesy Patidar Musli Farm, Jotpur (M.P.) Ph:07294-267251, 267351

SAFED MUSLI

Removing Soil from the Tubers

Cleaning of Tubers

A WHITE GOLD

With Courtesy Patidar Musli Farm, Jotpur (M.P.) Ph:07294-267251, 267351

SAFED MUSLI

Safed Musli at flowering stage

Mature Tubers

Tubers are kept in between soil in air cooled storage room for seeds

A WHITE GOLD

With Courtesy Patidar Musli Farm, Jotpur (M.P.) Ph:07294-267251, 267351

Current Scenario of Medicinal Plants in World

One can make the bold assertion that medicinal plants ought to be given the status of a national resource. This is because their sustained availability is essential to sustain one of world's oldest medical traditions, a priceless legacy of the Indian people. Millions of rural households use medicinal plants in a self-help mode. Over one and half million practitioners of the Indian Systems of Medicine, in the oral and modified streams use medicinal plants in preventive, promotive and curative applications.

It has estimated to be over 5000 manufacturing units in India with an annual turnover of over Rs. 4000 crores per year. In recent years, the growing demand for herbal product has led to a quantum jump in volumes of plant material traded within and across the countries. Conservative estimates put the economic value of medicinal plant related international trade to be of the order of US $ 880 million and this is growing. While the demand for medicinal plants is increasing, their survival in their natural habitats is under growing threat. Species like Coscinium fenestratum, Janakia arayalpathra, Dactylorhiza hatagirea, Saussurea costus are critically endangered in the wild.

It has presumed that around 1000 species of medicinal plants are facing threat to their existence in the wild, and some of them like Plectranthus vettiveroides have become extinct in the wild. It is not widely known that medicinal plants as a group comprise approximately 8000 species and account for around 50% of all higher flowering plant species of India. For a long-term and sustainable utilization programme for medicinal plants, it is imperative that medicinal plants are not only domesticated and put under cultivation, but also conserved in the wild.

The most cost-effective and a novel way to conserve and maintain the germplasm of medicinal plant is by establishing a network of insitu gene banks in the State forests. The insitu gene banks need to be located in relatively undisturbed forest reserves comprising areas of 200-500 ha size, located in different forest types and across the altitudinal range existing in the State.

Today, even the growing demands of the herbal products and the shrinking of forests, there is no option but there is an urgent need for cultivation of medicinal plants. Policy intervention is urgently needed to encourage and facilitate investments on commercial cultivation of medicinal plants.

It can be presumed that cultivated plants are likely to be somewhat different in their properties from those gathered from their natural habitats. Such differences can also be observed in the plants expression at different times of the same day, and in different seasons, at different stages of the plants growth and it is suggested in traditional literature even under different collections. On the other hand, scientists affirm that certain values in plants can be deliberately enhanced under controlled conditions of cultivation.

As a general policy "Polyculture" models for cultivation of medicinal plants where the species mix is based on natural associations, may be preferable to mono-culture cultivation. It is also advised to grow plants in their native agro-climatic locations and in habitats where they are naturally distributed.

Cultivation of medicinal plants is inversely linked to prevalence of easy and cheap collection from the wild, lack of regulation in trade, cornering of the profits from wild collection by a vast network of traders and middleman and absence of industry's interest in providing buy-back guarantees to growers. Cultivation of medicinal plants is also difficult due to lack of standardized agronomic practices for most species and unavailability of source of quality planting materials.

Policy measures to promote cultivation of medicinal plants, therefore need to facilitate industry's role by way of tax incentives etc. for investments in cultivation and agricultural research and simultaneously regulate indiscriminate, destructive collection of medicinal plants from the wild, while improving their conservation status *in situ*. In the context of medicinal plants, there is a special case for encouraging organic systems and polyculture models instead of the conventional monoculture models in agriculture and agro- forestry.

Even India's large population and food security needs, there is no way in which agricultural lands committed to food crops can be deviated to growing medicinal plants. Therefore a special case for encouraging in an "organized" way, small, marginal farmers and tribals to grow medicinal plants in their household gardens, bunds, wastelands rather than promoting a big farmer and large plantations strategy because this can encourage economic participation of the rural poor in the growth of the herbal industry.

One more important area for focused research is on the pharmacognosy of plants. With respect to plants used in indigenous systems of medicine, their "active compounds" cannot be inferred from traditional medical tests. The traditional advice related to potency of plants relates to their collection in particular seasons and from preferred habitats (Desh Vichar) and also to their specific biological activity expressed in terms of parameters like Rasa, Veerya, Guna, Karma etc. We need to, therefore, urgently develop creative pharmacognostic methods based on traditional knowledge because the current official standards are only related to the botany and chemistry of plants, but ignore their biological activity.

GLOBAL MARKET

According to the report of the World Health Organization (WHO), a large population of the world relies on the traditional systems of medicines, largely plant based to meet their primary health care needs. The EXIM bank of India, in its report has reported the value of medicinal plants related trade in India of the order of 5.5 billion US dollar and is growing rapidly. According to WHO, the international market of herbal products is estimated to be US $ 62 billion which is poised to grow to US $ 5 trillion by the year 2050. India's share in the global export market of medicinal plants related trade is less than 0.5%. The Chinese export based on plants including raw drugs, therapeutics and other is estimated to be around Rs. 18,000-22,000 crores. In view of the innate Indian strengths which interlay include diverse ecosystems, technical and farming capacity and a strong manufacturing sector, the medicinal plants area can become a huge export opportunity after fulfilling domestic needs.

Safed Musli (Chlorophytum borivilianum)

India is bestowed with a wealth of medicinal plants most of which have been used in Ayurveda, Unani systems of medicines and by tribal healers. Safed musli, a miraculous herb, ever known for countries and an alternative to chemical Viagra is scientifically known as *chlorophytum borivilianum* (Chloros – Green, Phytum-Plant) belongs to family liliaceae. It is also called as desi Viagra, plays a paramount role in Indian herbal medicine. The plant is being known for its use from ancient age. It grows naturally in the thick forests and nits use was confined to the tribals only. Nowadays with the efforts from research it can be cultivate at field level by following simple cultivation practices. It is an important herbaceous medicinal plant found in the forests of Madhya Pradesh and Gujarat states of India. But it is mainly distributed in Southern Rajasthan, North Gujarat and Western Madhya Pradesh. In nature, the plants grown in a wide range of places like open rocky places to shady and highly humus rich soil of the forest and require bright sunshine for better growth. The fleshy roots are the economically important part, which contain saponins and are used for the preparation of many Ayurvedic tonics prescribed against general debility. Dried roots of *Chlorophytum borivilianum* contains maximum amount of saponin, which ranges from 2-17%. It is thought to be highest in roots of Chlorophytum species, which are of forest origin. The content of saponin may be affected by the use of fungicides and synthetic pyrethroides. The roots of musli fetches an attractive market price, at present Rs. 900-1200 / kg of dry roots. In nature, the plant generates soon after or immediately before the rainy season (May-June) from the previous year's dormant root present in the soil. The stem is condensed to a disc from which it produces a whirl of leaves that are long, sessile and somewhat thick, emerge above the ground. The roots are fleshy and also sessile. The inflorescence is a receme and usually forms about one week after the sprout initiation, depending upon the stored food material in the roots, there may be two or three flowerings after the monsoon. Seeds germinate and give rise to plants, which rarely flower in the same year. However, 2-3% of the plants raised from seeds produced flowers in the experiments about 3 months after sowing. The plants are propagated vegetatively (by root having a portion of stem disc) for commercial cultivation as well as by seeds. However, seed germination percentage is very low (about 16%). Seeds have a dormancy period of about 8-9 months.

ORIGIN

The genus Chlorophytum includes about 300 species, which are distributed throughout the tropical and subtropical parts of the world. Tropical and subtropical Africa are the probable centre of origin of the genus, where about 85% of the species are found. The origin of Safed musli can be traced back in the oldest mountain ranges of the Indian continent, the ARAVALIS from where it spreads to the near-by areas of the sub continent.

VARIABILITY

Considerable morphological variability was observed in *Chlorophytum borivilianum* collections maintained at the National Research Centre for Medicinal and Aromatic plants. There are two distinct plant types were observed, i.e. prostrate or spreading type and erect type. In the prostrate type, the leaves come out from the stem disc and immediately spread out. Whereas in the erect type, the leaves (mainly the newly produced ones) grown upward for a short distance and then spread out. Leaf length, leaf breadth and maturity period also vary a lot in this species. Frequency of variability was seen in the case of root shape, size and colour. A plant type with variegated leaves was also identified. It was observed that the roots having blunt tip had better post harvest keeping quality than the tapering root tips. Correlation between morphological characters and chemical quality is under investigation. Vegetative propagation along with sexual reproductive in *C. borivilianum* helps to fix new variability in the population. However, unscrupulous collecting of these plants from the forests is posing a threat to its diversity. A serious effort is now required for the collection, preservation and maintenance of these variability. The National Research Centre for Medicinal and Aromatic plants has recently (in 1999) taken up a programme for collecting conservation and cataloging of *C. borivilianum* biodiversity under a World Bank funded National Agricultural Technology Project (NATP).

Different Species of Chlorophytum and their Distribution

	Species	Distribution
1.	*C. borivilianum*	Dangs Forests (Gujarat), Aravali hills
2.	*C. arundinaceum*	All districts of Chhota Nagpur, Vindhya, Satpura and Aravali hills, parts of central India, Tarai region of North-East Himalayas in Assam, West Bengal and Bihar
3.	*C. attenuatum*	Western Ghats, Southwards to Coimbatore, West Peninsula
4.	*C. laxum*	Katki hills, Belgaum, Dharwar, North and South Kanara, Deccan Peninsula in India.
5.	*C. tuberosum*	Parts of Konkan to Travancore in Kerala, Eastern Himalaya

	Species	Distribution
6.	*C. hreviscapum*	Bihar and West Bengal, Sikkim, Himalaya, Belgaum and South Peninsula.

DISTRIBUTION

It is widely distributed in India but not in other countries except Myanmar and China. In India it is widely distributed in Madhya Pradesh, North Gujarat and Southern Rajasthan. There are around 256 varieties of Chlorophytum in the world which are yet known, of which in India 7 species *viz.*, *Chlorophytum tuberosum*, *C. arundinaceum*, *C. breviscapum*, *C. attenuatum*, *C. laxum*, *C. borivilianum* and *C. malabaricum* are commonly observed.

All these species are totally different in medicinal properties. But due to lack of correct information all species are known as Safed musli in Indian drug market. Out of these seven observed species in the reputed books of Ayurveda, the plant mentioned as Safed musli is *Chlorophytum borivilianum*. It has got a good market demand both indigenous and globally. Due to the shy flowering as well as poor setting of viable seeds, the species has a very low rate of regeneration. For such a reason it may vanish from its known habits and thus may become a rare species. In view of this it is the need of the hour to stop large scale collection of this high value herb in forests with little efforts in order to bring it into regular cultivation. Thus it is must for one to have a complete know how of Safed musli.

DESCRIPTION

Floral Biology

The species *Chlorophytum borivilianum* is a small perennial herb with excess of radical leaves appearing over ground during the summer rain. The penetration occurs by fleshy roots or root tubers, which in turn are sessile and cylindrical of 1-8 in number. The leaves spread horizontally with rough lower surface and margins with parallel venation which are waxy. A solitary scape of 15-30 cm long is unbranched which bears flower over upper ¾ of its length. These flowers are white, arranged in alternate clusters each consisting of three flowers. The anthers are yellow, style is slightly longer than stamen, swollen at apex, ovary 3 lobed. Fruit is a loculicidal capsule, green to yellow triquestrous to sulcate with equal length and width. Seeds have onion like black appearance with angular edges.

Seed and Flower Formation

The question arises that what are the particular flowering features in Safed musli. To answer this query well developed plants with fleshy roots are to be planted both in nature as well as in the field. It has been observed that inflorescence is produced with the emergence of its sprouting within 4-6 days of receipt of first shower. However, from individual fleshy roots, if the plant is grown in field it has been observed that only fleshy root will produce inflorescence that are well developed but it may not have a good number of flowers. One inflorescence is produced by one plant but at a time 3-4 inflorescence has been observed which depends on the mother plant age or on the thickness and broadness of stem disc. Collection of seed has to be done with utmost care since all the capsules do not mature at the same time and moreover, dehiscence of capsule occurs as soon as it turns brown. For this reason one has to collect the seeds before the brown colour of the capsule appears. How should one collect the seed is another querry, one should collect the seeds in the field by bagging the inflorescence after setting of seeds and tying the lower end by V-pin or thread. Moreover, bags made up of butter paper with few pinholes are to be used for bagging of the inflorescence. It has been noted that 14-16 seeds bear one capsule.

Being a member of Liliaceae family it penetrates by fleshy roots attached to a condensed stem disc, which remains dormant in the soil for about 7 months. These are fascicled, sessile, cylindrical, variable in number and length, brown to black skinned and white after peeling.

Vernacular Names

Gujarat	:	Dholi musli
Marathi	:	Safed musli
Hindi	:	Safed musli
Malayalam	:	Shedheveli
Tamil	:	Taniravi Thang
Arabic	:	Shaqaqule
Sanskrit	:	Shweta musli
Telugu	:	Tella Nela Tadi Gaddalu
Oriya	:	Gaichira
Maharashtra	:	Safed or Sufeta musli
Kerala	:	Shedaveli
UP	:	Khiruva

Botanical Nomenclature

Safed musli belongs to the family Liliaceae, is a traditional medicinal plant found in natural forests right from Assam to Gujarat. It is a pretty herb of 1.5 feet height with erect lanceolate leaves and white coloured dense recemose type of inflorescence.

Nomenclature (Name)

Botanical	:	*Chlorophytum borivilianum*
Latin	:	*Chlorophytum arundinaceum*
Scientific	:	*borivilianum, arundinaceum, tuberocum, malabericum, attenuatum, breviscapum*
Common	:	Safed musli
Class	:	Monocotyledons
Series	:	Coronarieae
Genus	:	Chlorophytum
Species	:	borivilianum
Flowering	:	+ P (3+3) A 3+3, G White colour
Origin	:	Indian Subcontinent

PHYTO- CHEMISTRY OF SAFED MUSLI

Safed musli is rich source of over 25 alkaloids, vitamins, minerals, proteins, carbohydrates, steroids, saponins and polysaccharides etc. Research analysis has revealed that Safed musi roots consist of albumin but no starch as well as galacto glucan.

Table shows that chemical composition of Safed musli obtained from the market as well as samples of research laboratory. Furthermore, the dry tubers on analysis show various mineral composition such as:

Composition	Content (mg/g)
1. Sodium	0.04
2. Potassium	0.80
3. Calcium	6.5
4. Magnesium	1.9
5. Phosphorus	3.2
6. Zinc	0.002
7. Copper	0.148

Table 2. Chemical composition of market and research samples of Safed musli

S.N.	Contents	Research samples	Market samples
1.	Carbohydrates	42.00	38.10
a)	Reducing sugar	42.0	27.20
b)	Non reducing sugar	42.0	16.90
2.	Proteins	8.5	8.5
3.	Saponins	2.0-3.0	4.0
a)	Sugars	-	3.8
	i) Galactose	-	0.73
	ii) Glucose	-	0.76
	iii) Xylose	-	0.74
	iv) Arabinose	-	0.79
	v) Rhamnose	-	0.78
b)	Sapogenin (hecogenin)	0.17	0.16
4.	Aqueous Extracts	40	30
5.	Root fiber	3-4	2.0

Higher the saponin content, higher will be the medicinal properties. It is also mentioned in some prominent books of Ayurveda. The quality of saponin depends upon many factors. Generally, the Chlorophytum roots collected from forest are rich in saponin. It was also observed that under cultivation the saponin content goes down. The Chlorophytum roots having higher saponin content are having high demand in international drug market.

NEED FOR CULTIVATION

This plant is not new to the tribals of Madhya Pradesh, Gujarat and Rajasthan. They are using this medicinal plant from centuries. They use the fresh leaves of Chlorophytum as a potherb. According to survey the average foreign demand of chlorophytum roots is 300-700 tonnes annually. The heavy demand is creating a problem. The rate of demand for *Chlorophytum borivilianum* is even in higher side. Because of lack of information, Indian farmers are purchasing *C. arundinaceum* (inferior one) at the cost of *C. borivilianum* (superior one). In nature it is mainly propagated through roots and roots are the main economic part of this plant. Once the root is harvested from any place, the whole plant dies and reseeding never occurs at that place. So, due to commercial exploitation the availability of chlorophytum is decreasing and obnoxious weeds like Parthenium and Lantana are taking its place. Some of the main reasons for the commercial cultivation of musli are:

- Global demand for musli is necessiating the cultivation
- Forest was the only source, which is fast depleating since over exploitation hence cultivation is must
- As illustrated, Safed musli is a precious medicinal plant with expanding demand in domestic and international market.

Ethanobotany

Safed musli (*Chlorophytum borivilianum*) is an annual root crop, which has been traditionally consumed as a Vitalizer. It is an important ingredient of most of Ayurvedic medicines. Its extinction from forests has resulted in over exploitation. Besides, forest crop has been mixed and of poor quality, often maintained by tribal in unhygienic conditions. Now, this crop is not available in required quantity and quality, whereas demand for the crop is increasing as its properties have now been established.

Although for the traders, the roots of Safed musli are valuable part but for the traditional healers and natives of Chhattisgarh, India, its leaves are also important. They use it as potherb. Its use in the form of vegetable is very common and popular in almost every part of Chhattisgarh. The traditional healers and natives of different parts use the fresh leaves in different ways. The native uses the leaves as potherb possess unique medicinal properties and in many cases, this is more useful as compared to roots. The use of Musli leaves as potherb is also popular in Musli belts of other parts of India but its medicinal uses have not been reported. The traditional healers use this herb for the treatment of specific disease, they collect the leaves by adopting special worship ceremonies. The traditional healers and natives use both fresh and dry leaves of Musli. The traditional healers of Bastar region used the Musli leaves in combination with other herbs makes the human body enough resistant against the attack of sex related diseases. It is also used as medicine to delay the menopause, by the healers. Although the healers are aware of introduced species of Safed musli in Chhattisgarh but they prefer the use of native species for the preparation of herbal combinations. The herb collectors collect the Musli roots from forest at very immature stage because collection within three to four months after germination its life cycle complete and after fall or decaying of matured leaves, it is very difficult to locate the presence of Safed musli herb inside the soil, from ground level. It is common belief among scientific community that it is mere impossible to locate the Musli roots after the maturity and disappearance of aerial parts in forest floor having covered with fallen leaves of trees. Traditional healers use the tubers of Musli without peeling for the preparation of medicines

Uses of Safed Musli

In the Ayurvedic literature, Safed musli is celebrated as a Divya Aushad with unparalleled medicinal properties. It is a valued gift from the nature to human kind and chief ingredient in the preparation of over hundred Ayurvedic formulations. Besides its extensive use in Ayruveda and other conventional medicinal systems in Asia, Safed musli is also gaining increasing acceptance as a Vitalizer and health giving tonic. The roots of Safed musli contain a spermatogenetic, spermatorrhoea and chronic leucorrhoea due to some chemical contents. Apart from being a health tonic, it is remedy for erectile and orgasmic dysfunction also. Along side, the recent discovery of Safed musli as a natural and safe aphrodisiac agent has also opened up new channels of application and new demand for it. By virtue of being an herb, Safed musli has been found to be an ideal aphrodisiac with no negative side effects associated with chemical based aphrodisiac. Realizing it, the Gujarat State Forest Development Corporation has lately launched a Safed musli based potency drug named Nai Chetna, which is gradually gaining acceptance as a superior alternative to Viagra. Having passed adequate clinical trials, Safed musli will now be sold in the European and North American markets not as more food supplements like many of the Ayurvedic products, but as a registered medicine. Nowadays, there is a very vast demand all over the world specially Gulf countries and cold countries for Safed musli roots. Also in western India, especially in Gujarat, people are given to the habit of taking a spoon of Safed musli along with milk twice a day as a part of routine health care. There are also instances of Safed musli being used in various ways in varied parts of the country. That underlines the reason for a great deal of demand for Safed musli in India.

Following are the uses of Safed musli

1. As a principal ingredient in Ayurvedic, Unani and Allopathy application
2. As an aphrodisiac agent and Vitalizer
3. As a general sex tonic
4. As a curative for pre-natal and post-natal problems in women and useful for brain development in children.
5. As an effective safe alternative to Viagra
6. Acts as a restorative for immunity improvement
7. As a remedy for diabetes
8. As a curative for physical weakness and many illness
9. As a remedy for arthritis
10. Used in the preparation of new products like Nai chetana, Paurush, Chavanprash, Kauchapak, Painex (in North America)
11. Presently a number of health tonics (sexual tonics) are prepared from it
12. Used for increasing general body immunity
13. It has spermatogenic property and helpful in curing impotency as they are rich in glucosides
14. Curative of many physical illness and weakness
15. Above all these Safed musli is found very effective in increasing male potency.

Other uses of musli

- It is an essential part of a traditional diet of mothers (after delivery) in the form of "Laddoos"
- Used in PAN and GUTKHA
- Used in numerous Ayurvedic preparations and other uses mainly because it is a rich source of 25 alkaloids, vitamins, minerals, proteins, carbohydrates, steroids, saponins and polysaccharides etc.

Some of the herbal combinations containing Safed musli using as Sex tonic are:

1. Dry musli roots 5 gm along with dry asparagus racemosus roots 5 gm mix it and take it daily twice with fresh cow milk.
2. Dry musli roots along with dry Mucana seeds
3. Dry Echinops roots take it in equal amount, mix in zinger juice, make small pills (size of Zuzuba fruits) and take it daily morning with cow milk.
4. Even in many foreign countries researches are going on to prepare flakes, chips of Safed musli to use it as a nutritious break fast. Therefore Safed musli is being recognized as a high valuable herb among many herbs.

Cultivation Practices of Safed Musli

By virtue of being a forest plant, safed musli is sturdy and its cultivation is a simple and risk free task. There is a systematized approach to the cultivation of the plant to reap optimum yield and profits.

SOIL AND CLIMATE

Safed musli is a tuberous root crop, its development depends on the nature (texture) of the soil. It can be grown in different types of soils but sandy loamy soil is considered as best for musli cultivation. It is also grown in virgin soils and shoal soils. Soils rich in organic and humus content are ideal for growing the crop. Hard and clayey soils are not suitable for musli cultivation. The ideal soil pH for its cultivation should be 5.5 to 7.0 and it cannot tolerate alkalinity. Commercial part of the safed musli plant is its roots and these roots are growing underground. Therefore, the soil should be mellow. Apply super phosphate and decomposed farmyard manure (FYM) with good drainage system for its better tuber growth. Though no specific climate, soil and irrigation types can be prescribed for safed musli cultivation as it is naturally growing in different parts of India in various states having different soil types. It is even growing in the forests in natural conditions on soils having different pH and texture and at different altitudes. Heavy black soils are not suitable for its cultivation.

As musli grows naturally in most parts of central region of India, the normal climate of the central region suits the crop most and as per practical experience it can also grow successfully in the wide range of temperature and rainfall. Being its origin in southern part of Indian subcontinent, the plant grows well in tropical and sub-tropical climates with altitude upto 1500 meters. Climatic conditions such as warm and humid, in addition good amount of soil moisture during the growing season favours vegetative growth as well as facilitate fleshy root development. The species prefers the foot hills and warm moderate hill slopes. In Tamil Nadu, safed musli can be cultivated in the foot hills of western ghat hills and the eastern ghat hills. Warm humid weather throughout its life period is ideal for better yield. Cold regions of northern India are not ideal for its cultivation.

VARIETIES

Selections viz., RC-2, RC-16, RC-36, RC-20, RC-23, RC-37 and CT-1 are found to be good in terms of yield and saponin content. These varieties have been collected and maintained at RAU, Udaipur.

The other varieties of Safed musli which are high yielding, insect, disease and fungus resistant are MDB 13 and MDB 14.

LAND PREPARATION

Tractor drawn plough is used for deep cultivation followed by disc/cultivator harrowing to get fine tilth. Ploughing done in the month of March – April upto 1.5 to 2 ft depth and sowing of seeds of sunhemp (boru) or sesbania sp. (Dhaincha) at the rate of 60 kg per acre for green manure. Before commencement of flowers, sunhemp/ Dhaincha mixed with soil and irrigated for easy and early decomposition. If the area of cultivation is infested with termites than go for datura cultivation and mixed with soil. If soil is of clay nature and requires soil conditioning then use soil conditioner mycemeel (Hindustan Antibiotics, Pune) @ 1.5 ton/acre. Deep ploughing is done in the month of mid May and mixed 30-40 tonnes of decomposed FYM/acre. Besides FYM, application of neem cake @ 500 kg/ha also enhances the growth of tubers. For breaking of clods and better pulverization of soil go for 3-4 tillers. Then apply post emergence herbicide after 7 days of emergence of weed. Then wait for 7 days, irrigate and wait for 2nd emergence of weed. Then go for application of next post emergence herbicide.

After application of herbicide leave the land for one month for sowing. As a basal dose of DAP 120 kg ha^{-1} and MOP100 kg ha^{-1} are broadcasted before final land preparation and mixed uniformly with the top soil.

PREPARATION OF BEDS

1 Raised beds should be prepared as per planning of plantation at the end of May month

2 Like any tuberous species Safed musli could be better cultivated on raised bed

3 There is a tractor attachment accessible for raising the beds.

4 The beds are to be prepared along the slope of the land for proper surface water run-off

5 The beds are automatically raised with the help of special bed raiser to a height of 45 cm at the center, tapering to sides with a width of 105 cm and two beds are separated with 45 cm width of trench.

6 When beds are raised, half way through add 100 kg of single super phosphate, 50 kg of murate of potash, bone meal 100 kg, micro nutrients as per requirement are to be applied per

acre, only after the application of fertilizers the beds are to be raised to fullest height

7 Drip-lines are to be placed at the middle of the each raised bed.

8 The inline drippers are of 3 liters per hour capacity and placed 45 cm apart so as to wet the bed evenly

9 Final bed preparation activities must be completed before commencement of first rainfall (it depends on localities)

10 Safed musli cultivation requires raised bed for easy tuber growth for proper drainage

11 In case of flood irrigation system single line plantation bed must be made at the height of 20 cm with 30 cm distance between two single line plantation beds.

12 Single line beds could be easily irrigated manually by flood irrigation without any sprinklers or drippers

13 Weeding become easier between two single line beds by the tractor and weeding on the single line beds is also easier

14 All the raised beds should be well irrigated before sowing the planting material

IMPORTANCE OF RAISED BEDS

- Raised beds should prepared to facilitate better drainage of excess water and healthy growth of roots
- Size of these beds can be as per case and facility
- Size of the bed should be 1.05m width and 45 cm height
- Two beds should divided by 45 cm furrows
- These beds can be prepared by special implement of tractor.

SELECTION OF PLANTING MATERIAL

- For sowing, the tubers or fingers of musli are used
- Seed source could be collected from cultivated source
- Separate the sand and mud from the planting material (bunch of roots) purchased from the farm.
- From big bunch of planting material, bunch of 2-3 (fingers) roots could be separated (10 to 15g of each bunch) by a sharp operation blade carefully. So that a part of (crown) stem disc remains attached to each individual separated bunch of fleshy roots.
- The most important aspects of the best seeds are to have best considerable part of the disc or crown along with the seed.
- Care should be taken not to have any injury or damage to the tubers or skin.
- These (crown) stem discs are the most important portion and have direct role in vegetative propagation for bumper yield.
- Each finger should intact with some part of crown or disc, which is the germination point.

SEED TREATMENT

- Treat the bunch with growth harmones for better germination along with contact fungicide and bactericide to protect it from any kind of fungus.
- Seed should be treated with humicil @ 5 ml/l water and Dithane-M45 @ 5 gm/lit water for better results are found when tubers are treated with "GAU-MUTRA" (cow urine).
- Trichoderma viridae can also be used for tuber treatment.

SOWING

Safed musli is a kharif crop, it is sown in the month of June after first shower. Before planting deeply irrigate the field and after 3-4 days sowing (planting) should be done

- The complete yield depends upon the plantation of crop
- The planting material obtained from the digging process should be sown in the ready fields within two days
- At the time of sowing care should be taken to ensure adequate moisture in the soil
- While sowing (crown) stem disc part should be at the upper side and the (finger) tuber (non-crown part) should be at the down side and tuber should be in slanting position.
- These tubers should be planted 5cm deep with crown (stem disc) portion at upper side at a distance of 20cm and after planting, soil is to be covered by hand to prevent any damage
- Immediately after sowing (planting) irrigation should be given on the same day.

PROPAGATION

Safed musli is propagated through both seeds as well as by vegetative means i.e. fleshy root bearing shoot buds.

By Seeds

The colour of the seeds is black and they resemble onion seed in their shape and size having angular edges. Till June the seeds remain under dormant condition. Trials on the seed germination during July result in sprouting of seeds within 12-16 days in the trial plots. It has also observed that the percentage of germination in different cultures varies between 11 and 24%.

The seeds should be sown in a very well prepared seedbed, which is heavily manured by using FYM or leaf litter in the first or second week of June, and adequate moisture should be continuously maintained during absence of rain in early part of the season.

The seedlings can be transplanted in the field during the next kharif season only at 30 x 15 cm spacing because the development of plants as well as roots by means of seeds in the first year is not vigorous enough as compared to vegetatviely propagated plants.

By Vegetative Means

The fleshy roots bearing short buds starts the initiation of sprouts in the mid May in stored material under laboratory conditions. However, in the forests within 4-6 days after the receipt of rain, from the ground the seedlings emerge.

However, if one has to raise the plants in the field for such a purpose either the sprouted seedlings under lab conditions has to be collected with in 10-30 days after the receipt of rains and simultaneously transplanted in the field or the fleshy root bunches should be taken out from the ground or from storage place in mid of May and it should be mixed with same amount of moist soil (1-2%) thereby keeping them in ploythene bags that are perforated and having a capacity of 1 kg. Care should be taken to keep these bags in a cool place and the bags mouth should be tight. Moreover, the seed buds must remain adhered to the slim disc portion.

The fleshy roots of musli produces more vigorous plants by vegetative propagation than by the seeds because of readily available stored food material in the fleshy root, which supports initial growth. Further, the vegetative propagation produces three times more yield of fleshy roots over the crop raised by seeds. Even a small 1 cm long and slightly fleshy roots or rootstock has a capacity to reproduce into new plants. These fleshy roots sprout form second week of May to second week of June. The sprouted fleshing propagules should be planted in the field in first or second week of June, fallowed by irrigation. The practice of planting on top of the ridges of 15-20 cm height at a row distance of 30x15 cm is found ideal for obtaining commercial yield.

GROWTH OF THE SEED

Monsoon starting with thunders is responsible for sprouting of the tubers and the plant emerges in about 10 days, flowering begins on 15th day and the leaf part grows to its maximum by 70 days. It matures by 120 days as the leaf-fall starts. The tubers are continues to retain 4 months in the soil even after the leaf fall they should not plucked as changes occur. The tubers get the cuticle layer on the finger and there is an intake of material from soil to the tuber till 9 months.

SPACING

Tubers with disc are planted on raised beds at a spacing of 30 cm between the rows and 25 cm between the plants. Also, the spacing of 20 cmx20cm is suitable for its better growth.

On the basis of research carried out at Akola (Maharashtra), the significant effect of plant population was noticed on length of tubers fresh and dry yield of tubers. The fresh and dry yield of tubers was significantly highest due to population (30x10 cm) on the contrary tuber length and yield per plant was move with the population of 1.66 lakh (30x20 cm).

SEED RATE

It requires a seed rate of 400-500 kg of seed tubers. Nearly 30000-35000 fingers are required per acre.

IRRIGATION

Water management plays a vital role in musli cultivation. Care should be given to keep the soil moist until it germinates from planting. Irrigation is given at 8 to 10 days interval, however it depends on prevailing weather. Light irrigation is needed until harvest even after drying and falling of leaves. Use of sprinkler or drip method of irrigation is advisable for better results incase of wider. Attention should be paid while irrigating the land because standing of water for long period affects the crop growth and favour fungal infection and ultimately it hinders production. After leaves dry and leaf fall down from stem the irrigation should be given at 15 to 20 days interval. In case of long periods of no rainfall, irrigation is necessary to maintain moisture in the soil for healthy growth of the plant and the tubers.

DETOPPING

It is one of the operation in cultivation of musli, the sprouted tubers grown and flower. The inflorescence arise from the base of the plant should be removed to encourage the tuber bulking.

MANURES AND FERTILIZERS

Musli cultivation requires different kinds of fertilizers like FYM, chemical fertilizers, green manures and micro nutrients for better profit of the crop.

Farm Yard Manure (FYM)

It is very essential since it enhances water holding capacity and fertility of the soil. 10 to 15 tons of well decomposed manure is applied per acre area of land.

Green Manures

Green manuring is vital to improve the fertility of the soil. Ideal sources of green manure are Sesbania, Crotalaria or Jammu and Pillipesara.

Chemical Fertilizer

Though application of chemical fertilizers favour the crop growth, it is advised not to go for heavy application considering the importance at international markets. Minimum dose of 20 kg N, 40 kg P_2O_5 and 20 kg K_2O per acre is recommended. Basal dose of fertilizer should be applied at the time of planting. After 45 days of planting second dose should be applied by fertilizer injection method (stamping).

Micronutrients

Bone based multi micro nutrient fertilizers (Golden) is available in the market, which can be mixed @ 5 bags (50 kg) per acre. Micro nutrient tonics are also used for foliar spray. In case of zinc deficiency application of 10 kg $ZnSO_4$ is ideal for its growth.

For a tuber species like Safed musli an application of bone meal provides phosphorus and the necessary micronutrients.

ORGANIC FARMING

Application of 20-25 tonnes of FYM and 2-4 tonnes of vemicompost are applied every year. Application of one ton of gypsum is recommended as soil amendment. Spraying and spot drenching of phachakavya at 15day interval can help in increasing the soil health and promote the growth and yield of musli. Application of neem cake @ 500 kg ha^{-1} also enhances the growth of tubers.

On the basis of research carried out at Akola (Maharastra), it has found that application of organic manures had beneficial effect on yield of safed musli. It is also observed that the number of tubers and steroidal sapogenine content was found to increase with the addition of organic manures through both the sources viz. FYM and vermicompost. The steroid content was significantly highest due to application of vermicompost @ 5 tonnes ha^{-1}.

WEED MANAGEMENT

- Regular weeding is necessary for proper and healthy growth of the safed musli
- The weeding should be done timely, use of chemical herbicides is not advisable.
- Before weeding irrigate the field properly a day before for easy hand weeding
- For control of weeds at least 2-3 weeding to be done in 30-40 days.
- Weeding must be done on the raised beds by manual labours

NUTRITIONAL DEFICIENCIES

Iron deficiency in soil leads to chlorosis. Initially chlorosis of young leaves followed by gradual necrosis.

Correction measure: Spray ferrous sulphate once in 2 months

PLANT PROTECTION

The leaf of musli is to be protected from any kind of diseases and pests for better yields. Musli being in the form of tubers is underneath the ground and hence, free from natural disasters like heavy showers. The drainage system has to be well prepared to avoid water logging and the damage of tubers. Water stagnation is avoided because it favours fungal development on tubers. Generally musli is free from pest and diseases, except some fungi like Rhizoetonia, Fusarium species for which fungicides may used.

Pests like leaf eating caterpillars, white grubs and disease like leaf blight and red spot are observed, which can be controlled by following timely plant protection measures.

Rotting of roots during storage can be controlled by treatment with Thiram and Captan at 4.0 grams per kg of roots.

Disease like anthracnose mainly caused by Colletotrichum spp. Dark brown to brownish black spots on leaves will appear.

Control measure: spray Bavistin or Benomyl (0.15%) at the time of first appearance of the disease

INTER CROPPING

Musli can be cultivated as an inter crop with mango, teak, neem, paulownia, Amla and Sapota (Chiku) etc. with remarkable results. It can also be intercropped with papaya, banana and maize.

HARVESTING

The crop matures in about 90 days under cultivation. Seed formation activities started from maturation of flowers and seed maturation (yellowing of capsule and black coloured seed like onion seeds) completed within 2-3 months and simultaneously fresh tuber formation will also start. After the leaf fall, the tubers are to be left in the ground and should not be taken out, as changes occur in the tuber that will increase the value of the tuber. At the time of leaf fall, the tubers are light in colour and as they mature by time, they become deep black. At leaf fall stage (90 DAS) the tubers are not hardy, thin and smooth skin with high water percentage (about 85-90%). These tubers are not suitable for next year planting, for that purpose the tubers are left in the soil upto eight months. This process will come down the water content of the tuber 70-75% and increase the hardiness of the tubers. Before going for harvesting, the field should be properly irrigated for easy and safe dig out of tubers. Safed musli bunch is to be dug out by manual labour or by ploughing very carefully to prevent damage to the crown (disc) or to the tubers (fingers) while digging. The digging operation manually from the ground requires around 60-70 men per day for one acre of land area.

STORAGE OF PLANTING MATERIAL

- The harvested bunch of roots should be collected with sand stick and heap in the shade.
- The heap is stirred at 3-4 days interval for next 8 to 12 days
- Make the harvested bunch free from sand and mud by cleaning with clean water.

- Fleshy roots should be separated from the bunch by slight pressure of the fingers and thumb on each root, which will separate the root from the main bunch.

- Ventilated racks are used to store musli tubers for next year in controlled temperature of 25-31°C and at a relative humidity of 50-65 per cent.

YIELD

In one acre 80,000 plants are planted and more than 70,000 will survive upto the harvest. If one plant weight even 30 gram, from one acre area 2100 kg (21qt) fresh tuber can be obtained and it gives about 400-500 kg of dry musli.

Estimation of Cost of Cultivation for Five Acre Land Area

	(Rs. in Lakh)
I YEAR –NURSERY YEAR – INPUTS	
a) Cost of the plantation material (@ 500 kg/acre) @ Rs. 400 per Kg for 2,500 Kg of Tubers	10.00
b) Cultivation Expenses @ Rs. 75,000 per acre for 5 Acres	3.75
• Land preparation	
• Fertilizers & Chemicals	
• Irrigation	
• Labour charges	
Expected output- 1 year	
a) 10,000 kg of sowable Musli (Worth about Rs. 40 lakhs)	
b) 2500 kg of broken material becomes 500 kg (20% of weight on drying)	
Sale price of dry Musli @ Rs. 1000 per kg	5.00
	8.75
II YEAR-BREAK –EVEN YEAR - INPUTS	
• 10,000 kg of planting material for 20 acres	8.75
• Cultivation expenses @ Rs. 60,000 per Acre	12.00
	20.75
Expected output – II year	
40, 000 kg of sowable Musli (80 acre)	

	(Rs. in Lakh)
10, 000 kg of broken material (tubers)	
50,000 kg -20% dry Musli (total on drying) – 10,000 kg	
10,000xRs. 1,000/-= Rs. 1,00,00,000 (One Crore)	100.00
TOTAL	**79.25**

- Prices as per the Prevailing market
- Multiplication of tubers depends on proper implementation of package of practices, proper land preparation, weed and pest management, moisture in the soil and careful harvest.

From the above economics, it is obvious that Safed musli is a high-potential commercial crop with huge returns on investment. Going by the above calculations, an investment of Rs. 25 lakh in the cultivation of 5 acres of Safed musli in the first year, followed by 25 acres of cultivation of in second year, will fetch a whopping return of Rs. 1 crore in just two years. The yet another attendant benefit of Musli cultivation is a 100% tax exemption.

Calendar of Operation

It is nothing but a graphic or tabular presentation showing the kinds of operations to be performed during the seasons and specified time limits within which work must be done.

20th September	Irrigate the land, deep ploughing and draw the cultivator
1st October	Boardcast green manuring seeds like sun hemp, @ 35-40 kg/acre
20th October	Apply 50 kg of DAP/acre
25th November	Incorporation by green manuring crop
27th November	Irrigate the field
10th February	Deep ploughing
20th of February	Draw cultivator
1st March	Adding compost @ 20 tons/acre
3rd March	Draw cultivation
2nd Week March	Drip Installation
25th March	Bed preparation
30th March	De-thermification
2nd April	Sowing

Export Potential

- International market for medicinal plants is of the order of US$800 million per year. The botanical market inclusive of herbs and medicinal plants in the US is estimated at US$ 1.6 billion per year. Due to increasing patronage of herbal-based health products in the USA, Europe and many countries, Safed musli gained unmatched prospects for the commercial cultivation.

- Europe imports about 4,00,000 tonnes of medicinal plants per annum, with an average market value of US $1 billion from Africa and Asia.

- Japan has the highest per capita consumption of botanical medicines in the world.

- There are many enquiries for 'A' Grade dry Safed musli from various Gulf European countries.

- Increasing Global demand for aphrodisiac medicines with no side effects, Safed musli has immense potential to become a key curative for erectile and organic dysfunctions.

- The economics of Safed musli varies due to rate of planting material, market rate of dry musli and the system of sowing and production etc. In normal conditions the economics can be estimated as fallows for a five acre area of land in successive years.

Organic Farming in Safed Musli

The commercial cultivation of herbal species requires intensive care and management. Though the package of practices for many medicinal plants have not been studied and documented, organic cultivation is preferable since there is demand only for organically grown species. The conventional chemical farming system may lead to the problem of deterioration of quality of the active principle. It can be nullified only through the organic cultivation methods. Hence, the WTO agreement also pushes the growers to cultivate the medicinal plants by organic methods to improve their income. In addition, organically grown medicinal plants can get the premium price of even up to three fold of normal price.

COMPONENTS OF ORGANIC FARMING

Green Manuring

Legume crops like cowpea, sunhemp, daincha in plains and lupin in hilly tracts of Nilgiris can be grown as cover crops/intercrops in medicinal plants cultivation and can be incorporated in to the soil as manure; Apart from fixing atmospheric nitrogen, incorporation of the biomass provides additional nitrogen 50-60 kg ha^{-1}.

ANIMAL DUNG/POULTRY MANURE

In order to enhance the soil fertility vis-à-vis productivity of land in use, periodical application of organic manures through animal dung was traditionally practiced. The application of organic manures @ 25 kg/ha may be made as basal.

COMPOST

The well decomposed biodynamic compost should be applied @ 5 t/ha.

Panchagavya

Panchagavya an organic preparation was evaluated as foliar spray and soil drenching in cultivation of Safed musli. The results revealed that the foliar spraying and soil drenching of 3% panchagavya improve the growth and yield of Safed musli. The panchagavya is prepared with the following ingredients:

Cow dung	:	7 kg
Cow urine	:	10 litre
Water	:	10 litre

After 15 days, the following ingredients shall be added.

Cow milk	:	3 litre
Cow curd	: :	2 litre
Cow ghee	:	1 litre
Tender coconut water	:	3 litre
Jaggery	:	3 kg (or)
Sugarcane juice	:	3 litres
Banana	:	12 nos.

The ingredients should be mixed thoroughly both in the morning and evening and in twenty-five days the panchakaviyam is ready for spray. 3% solution (3 ml in 100 ml) should be sprayed to the medicinal plants 12 times at 10 days interval will increase the yield and give resistance for pests and diseases. Panchakaviya 3% solution as seed treatment also found to break dormancy in hard seed coated plants.

BIO-FERTILIZERS

Bio-fertilizers are microbial inoculants, which are capable of nitrogen fixation and phosphorate solubilisation.

Azotobacteria/ Azospirillium Inoculants

It is an important group of non-symbiotic N fixing bacteria. It also promotes growth of plant by helping in the synthesis of auxins, vitamins and growth substances.

These can be applied as basal dosage @ 2.5 kg/ha.

Phosphate Solubilizing Micro-organisms

The group of organism of *Phosphobacterium* help to solubilizing insoluble form of phosphorus in the soil and make it more available to the plant. They also synthesize growth promoting substances useful for the plants. These can be applied as basal dosage @ 2.5 kg/ha.

Arbuscular Mycorrhizae (AM)

Micorrhizae is found in symbiotic association between plant roots and fungal mycelia. The fungi infect plant roots and spread inside them through structure called as arbuscules, which help in the transfer of nutrients from the fungus to the plant roots. This association helps to increase absorption of nutrients by plants as well as induce disease resistance. This can be applied at the time of preparation of seedling beds of medicinal plants nursery @ 10 g/sq.m.

Vermicompost

Vermicompost is yet another organic manure, born out of the process of recycling organic wastes into nutrient rich compost and the earthworms, know as farmers friend, are the agents for undertaking this recycling process.

Earthworms are known to live in the soil upto three meter depth, thus increasing porosity, aeration and infiltration. Apart from improving the physical features of soil they contribute to bringing about favourable chemical changes. The vermin-castings contain the excreta, cocoons and undigested feed form excellent organic manure. It is estimated that about 750 kg of vermicompost can be prepared from one pit of size 2x1x1m in a period of 2 months form 1000 kg of wastes. The vermicompost contains about 0.72 per cent nitrogen, 0.25 per cent phosphorous and 2.74 per cent of potassium.

All the physiologically active water soluble components of vermicompost such as humic acids, plant growth regulators, amino acid, vitamins, micro nutrients and microbial cells are extracted in water and is known as vermiwash. The water soluble components from vermicompost may be collected by passing water slowly through the worm beds or by simple suspension of vermicompost in water. This is used for foliar applications as such or after sufficiently diluting, based on the need. The foliar application of vermiwash once in month found to improve the growth, yield and quality of the Safed musli.

BIOCONTROL AGENTS

The Rhizobacteria viz., *Pseudomonas fluorescens* and *Bacillus subtilis* and the fungus *Trichoderma viride* are the promising biocontrol agents used for the management of plant diseases. The commercial formulation of these biocontol agents have been developed at Horticultural Research Station, Ooty. The *Pseudomonas fluorescens* is recommended as 5% foliar spray, soil application (2.5 t/ha) and seedling root dip (5% solution) for the control of leaf spot and wilt diseases. The *Trichoderma viride* is recommended as seed treatment (4 g/kg) and soil application (2.5 kg/ha) for the control of root rot and wilt diseases.

Homa Farming (Agni Hotra ash)

Agni Hotra ahs is the by-product of Homa farming practice called Agni Hotra, which is prepared by burning dry cow dung, cow ghee, unbroken raw rice in inverted copper pyramid at sunrise and sunset. It was believed that adoption of Homa farming in agricultural field completely sterilized the environment and cleared the field from pathogens. The experiments conducted at Horticultural Research Station, Udhagamandalam (Ooty), revealed that effect of foliar spraying of Agni Hotra ash (200 g of Agni Hotra ahs in 1 lit. cow urine kept for 25 days for fermentation and it dissolved in 10 liter water) was highly effective in the control of leaf spot diseases. Hence, the same practice may be followed in cultivation of medicinal plants.

BIODYNAMIC ORGANIC FARMING

The Biodynamic method is more than just another organic method, which will speed up the developmental process of organic farming. Biodynamic agriculture can otherwise also be called as a "Horticultural farming system". It encourages the mixed farming with animal husbandry as an important component. Mean while it insists all organic principles, mainly on green manuring, crop rotation, compost making and its application and natural way of controlling the insects and pest incidence. Apart from these, it emphasizes very much on the utilization of the cosmic forces and the effect of moon rhythms in farming by proper planning of all garden activities using the planting calendar. This farming system can be practiced in organic farming system only.

Biodynamic preparations

Horn Manure .... : .... BD 500
Horn Silica .... : .... BD 501

Compost preparations

Yarrow .... : .... BD 502
Chamomile .... : .... BD 503
Stinging Nettle .... : .... BD 504
Oak Bark .... : .... BD 505
Dandelion .... : .... BD 506
Valerian.................. : .... BD 507

Contract Farming in Safed Musli

Commercial cultivation of medicinal plants in India is restricted to only very few crops. The economically developed countries been able to revive interest in medicinal plants and exploit this for social and economic advantage. It is mainly because of the following factors:

- Sustained and well-focused scientific (R&D) research has been carried out to verify the traditional claims and also establish their safety. For instance, there have been more than 350 studies on *Echinacea* spp., over 200 publications on St. John's wort. Several aspects of work on ginkgo have been collected in two volumes covering over 160 articles.
- Secondly, the above effort was reinforced by complementary national legislations. In Germany, phyto-medicines are classified by law as drugs, and hence have to meet the same stringent criteria of quality, efficacy, and safety as obtains for the usual clinical drugs. In order to monitor these products, German Government's Commission has, by now, produced 380 monographs on 190 herbs and fixed combinations, approved for therapeutic use.
- Finally, for commercial success of any plant-based product it is imperative that sustained supply of plant material is in place. In several cases, the concemed parties have gone in for scientific farming of required medicinal plant. For example, there is a huge (10 million trees) plantation of

ginkgo near Sumter, SC, USA for catering to the needs of European manufacturers of ginkgo leaf extract.

In order to improve our herbal market, the focus should be on proper herbal production system and to work out an ideal and organized system to capitalize the international market like China. Medicinal plants can be mainly grown under four major farming systems:

- Contract farming
- Corporate farming
- Group farming
- Cooperative farming

Among these systems Safed musli is one of the commercial medicinal herb grown under contract farming at many places of our country.

CONTRACT FARMING

Today most small farmers around the world are independent producers who sell their produce individually and have little bargaining power with suppliers or markets. But farmers and agribusinesses are increasingly linking up in mutually beneficial arrangement. This method of production is called as contract farming. In this farming, farmers and processing firms agree before seeds are sown as to what crops the farmer will grow and often, the price of the firm will pay for the resulting harvest. This protects farmers from market fluctuations and guarantees that processors have adequate supplies of the produce they need. Contract farming is in practice in the field of medicinal herbs, poultry, livestock and dairy industries. This method of farming is already in existence in our country and majority of the medicinal plant grown commercially are marked in this way.

For any medicinal plants to be cultivated under contract system, the following requirements have to be met.

- Demand for the particular species
- Species should have high volume of requirement (domestic or abroad)
- Buyers to purchase the raw materials
- Availability of large extent of suitable cultivable land in one region
- Species should be remunerative than the conventional crops
- Shorter in duration and less labour requiring

Practical Implications

- Demand for particular species is not static/continuous which results in abrupt cancellation of orders
- Sudden shift in usage
- Development of cheap alternate resource

Factors to be Considered for Refining the Contract Farming

1 State level monitoring of demand and supply,

2 Government level production controlling authority like China

3 Protection of farmers/local tribes

4 Financial assistance from Bank like any other conventional crops

5 Options of Crop Insurance

6 Legal implications when demand drops suddenly

The Role of Companies in Contract Farming

1 The pharmaceuticals and herbal companies can provide credit plans for the farmers

2 They can offer cultivation practices of medicinal plants

3 They can supply quality-planting materials

4 They can conduct training programmes for the farmers

5 They can assist the growers in finding suitable market and prices for the medicinal plants

6 The companies can help the farmers in expanding the areas of medicinal plants under cultivation

7 The companies can provide the agro-consultancy services like soil identification, seed and planting material supply, pest management, post harvesting technologies and the necessary market linkage.

The companies shall disseminate the latest farm technology and distribution network for local and export consumption of medicinal plants.

The Role of Farmers in Contract Farming

The following are the roles that the farmers shall play in contract farming of medicinal plants.

1 The farmers shall raise the medicinal plants required by the companies.

2 Follow the agro-techniques provided by the companies strictly.

3 Supply the produce in time to the companies.

4 The farmers can form either self-help group or co-operatives or growers associations to protect their interest.

The Success Stories of Contract Farming in India

The Success of Eucalyptus

The paper and the rayon mills are meeting their Eucalyptus raw materials in India mostly from the farmers supply. The social forestry projects in many states helped the farmers to raise and supply Eucalyptus to the companies by contract farming. The companies initially supplied the enough credit and seedlings to the farmers and bought the Eucalyptus from the farmers for the agreed price.

The Success of Poplars

The success of poplars in northern India is another example for contract farming. The Wimco Company has entered into agreement with the farmers for the supply of pulpwood. The farmers and the company took it as a joint venture and both of them meet their requirements for so many years.

The Success of Contract Farmings in Basmati Rice

In Punjab, Government Company, Punjab Agro-industrial Corporation and LT Overseas have entered into an agreement to cultivate bas mati rice through contract farming for more than 10,000 hectares. The farmers will receive financial assistance from the financial institutions with the help of the companies.

The Success of the Contract Farming in Wheat

In Madhya Pradesh the Hindustan Lever Ltd has gone for contract farming of w)1eat.

The Success of the Contract Farming in Cotton

The Appachi Cotton Company in Tamil Nadu has entered into an agreement with the Tibetan Cotton farmers in Karnataka for the supply of cotton for the companies in Tamil Nadu.

The contract farming in medicinal plants cultivation has started now in a small scale. If both the companies and farmers take it seriously, it would become a good success.

The Medicinal Plants Recommended for Contract Farming

	Botanical Names	Common Names
1	*Aloe vera.*	Kumari.
2	*Andrographis paniculata*	Kalmegh
3	*Asparagus racemosus*	Shatavari.
4	*Chlorophytum borivillianum*	Safed Musli
5	*Coleus forskhol/ii*	Coleus
6	*Crocus sativus*	Saffron
7	*Gloriosa superba*	Kalihari
8	*Gymnema sylvestre*	Gudmar
9	*Ocimum sanctum*	Thulasi
10	*Piper longum*	Pippal
11	*Plantago ovata*	Isabgol
12	*Rauwolfia serpentina*	Sarpagandha
13	*Solanum nigrum*	Makoy
14	*Tinospora cordifolia*	Giloe
15	*Withania somnifera*	Ashwagandha

Benefits of Contract Farming

- Demand could be met
- Supply within the stipulated time.
- Prior agreement helps in legal protection to farmers
- Better remuneration to farmers if agreement is proper
- Maintenance of uniform quality

Problems Anticipated in the Contract Farming

The companies may not pay the farmers the price agreed upon by both of them while entering into agreement. Similar way, the farmers may not deliver the produce to the companies in time as per the agreed terms and conditions.

This problem can be easily overcome by constituting a committee having members from the company, farmers and the government representatives. The committee can decide the market price at the time of delivery of the produce and offer more rates to the farmers than the agreed price if the market price is higher. If the market price is found to be lower than the agreed price, the committee will ensure the companies offered the agreed price to the farmers without any loss to the companies. This type of arrangement is working well with the Food, Fats and Fertilizer Ltd, Koppal in Karnataka for the contract farming of oil palms.

CORPORATE FARMING

Corporate farming is a farming system wherein corporate, public and multinational companies involve in promotion of medicinal plant cultivation on a corporate scale. Under such system, the corporate enter agreement with the multinational processing companies for supply of raw materials or the herbal extracts. A striking example of this system is turmeric, where multinational companies procure huge quantities of raw material, process the rhizomes and export the extracted oleoresins and alkaloids to pharmaceutical companies of the world.

In India, this system helps in opening of new avenues for employment of the rural folk in organized sector. Under this system, there will be opportunities for employment, people participation which could lead to a better life and security for employment, health and educational facilities and a general upliftment in their social status. Agricultural holdings will remain intact and will not disintegrate with the passing of generations. Agricultural operations will thus be carried on in a most economic and profitable manner. This might be an example for land owners to join together and develop agriculture on commercial lines.

- Science and Technology Entrepreneurs Park (STEP) of the IIT, Kharagpur joined hands with Aditya Biotech Pvt Ltd for a medicinal plants project at Gopali, Kharagpur
- Aditya Biotech stipulates that the medicinal plants should be grown on land owned by STEP with its technical know how
- Aditya would operate all expenses for the project
- Currently Safed musli, Sarpaganda, Aloe vera, Brahmi and Kalmegh are grown
- 20 % of gross revenue would go for STEP
- 100 % of land is utilized

COOPERATIVE FARMING

The functioning of Co-operatives in the country is far from satisfactory. They are also inhibited by several constraints which will hamper rapid growth. In China, Ginseng, Cooperators is an informal association for people and wild herbs. Harvesters, Wildcrafters and Diggers practice good conservation and offer their products to customers on the internet.

In India this farming system is more applicable and many such co-operative societies functioning for several crops especially horticultural crops are found to be more successful and applicable. In Tamil Nadu the state level co-operative society *viz.*, TANHERB, the Tamil Nadu Medicinal Herbs Cultivators, Processors, Manufacturers and Research Industrial Co-operative Society Ltd has initiated several measures for the protection of farmers from middlemen in marketing the herbal raw materials. The society is a registered one functioning under the control of the Ministry of Industries and Commerce at Madurai and has around 500 members.

GROUP FARMING

Groups of small-scale farmers can increase their productivity, profits and bargaining power by joining with other similar groups. These associations are important where small-scale farmers can acquire new skills in the management of larger organizations. Such groups can also serve as useful development vehicles, not only helping farmers solve their own problems but making it easier for governments to assist them in their efforts.

Forming of small farmer group associations and networks, shows how, using a participatory approach, inter-group associations can be established in rural areas capitalizing the herbal cultivation in a proper way. Small farmer group development is intended for use by group promoters, extension workers and other rural development staff to help existing farmer associations to join forces and run inter-group enterprises.

Group farming is applicable for permanent development activities like conservation of rare species of indigenous medicinal plants through community participation for better health and environment. In India, group participation comes under the umbrella of NGO's, self help groups, several welfare associations. The Bangalore based NGO, FRLHT, has taken a lead in conservation and development of medicinal plants in India. FRLHT, a non governmental organization which was established in 1991, is dedicated to the cause of revitalization of India's rich and diverse health traditions that includes:

- Strengthening Local Health Traditions in rural communities

- Conservation and sustainable utilization of medicinal plants including promotion of small scale medicinal plant enterprises for generation of income and employment for rural communities.
- Dissemination of medicinal plants related knowledge drawn from traditional and modern knowledge systems and including market information
- Research on selected medical, sociological and epistemological aspects of Indian Medicinal Heritage.

FRLHT has initiated a pioneering collaborative program since 1993, in collaboration with the state Forest Departments, local NGOs, local communities and Research institutes. A network of over 50 conservation sites have been established in the Western and Eastern Ghats. These sites are located across the states of Kerala, Tamilnadu, Karnataka, Andhra Pradesh and Maharastra. This network is the largest post-independent effort for the conservation of medicinal plants and is called as "Medicinal plant Conservation Network" (MPCN). The network aims to conserve medicinal plants. The MPCN is today conserving about 1400 species of medicinal plants, including 70 RED-listed species.

Micro Propagation Studies in Safed Musli

In vitro propagation of rare Indian medicinal herb "Safed musli" (*Chlorophytum borivilianum*) was achieved using encapsulated shoot buds. Four millimeter long shoot buds encapsulated in 3% sodium alginate matrix polymerized by 100 mM solution of $CaCl_2$. $2H_2O$ yielded best results. Storage conditions get matrix media and period in storage influenced the *in vitro* regrowth potential of shoot buds when transferred on standard multiplication (SM) medium containing MS salts and 5.0 mg IBAP. Encapsulated shoot buds stored on wet agar-gel and kept under culture room conditions of light and temperature (45 μmol m sand 28A±2°C, respectively) showed more than 80% sprouting within 3 weeks. Dark stored (4°C) encapsulates shoot buds on agar-gelled wet medium showed more than 90% sprouting after 7 days of storage. The per cent response in terms of regrowth potential declined to 60% when buds were stored for more than 30 days attaining a low of 20% in another 30 days. Supplementing alginate matrix with sucrose and MS salts (ALMSS) produced better results as compared to that with MS salts alone (ALMS) or without any of them (ALW). All the sprouted shoots, buds, irrespective of their storage conditions, produced normal shoots of SM and multiplied at the rate of 2.5 fold per subculture of 21 d each. More than 70% micro shoots could be rooted on the medium containing ¾ MS salts and 2.0 mg IIBA. Rooted plants were hardened successfully and grown under greenhouse conditions where they produced normal shoots on SM and multiplied at the rate of 2.5 fold per subculture of 21 d each. More than 70% micro shoots could be rooted on the medium containing ¾ MS salts and 2.0 mg IIBA. Rooted plantlets were hardened successfully and grown under greenhouse conditions where they produced normal tuberous roots. This method of micropropagation opens possibilities for storage of shoot buds during off-season of production and facilitate transport of germplasm with ease.

Constraints in the Cultivation of Safed Musli

1. LACK OF RELIABLE AND COMPLETE PACKAGE OF PRACTICES

The package for the cultivation of Safed musli is mainly developed by the private organizations and farms. These packages are not standardized one and also farmers have to pay more money for getting these packages. So these packages are beyond the reach of our farmers. Now there is an urgent need that the government organizations like agricultural universities and other research institutes should come forward for taking up research on the agrotechniques of valuable crops like Safed musli.

2. LACK OF IMPROVED VARIETIES AND RELIABLE PLANTING MATERIAL

Genetically superior varieties are really the hub of all activities related to scientific and organized cultivation of crop. It has been noted that the availability of planting material of improved varieties in bulk and reliable planting material is the major constraint in cultivation.

In several important medicinal plants, genetically stable and high yielding varieties with better quality end products are yet to be developed. Only wild bulk are under cultivation. Poor yield and quality of industrial raw material is the obvious result influencing the interest of growers and user industries.

3. LACK OF ORGANIZED MARKETING

Inspite of regular internal demand and growing export, the trade in this sector is largely unorganized. Growers in non-traditional areas have limitations to readily dispose of their produce, as buyer prefers to collect the raw material from traditional areas of cultivation.

4. MARKET FLEXIBILITY AND LACK OF ASSURED BUY BACK

There is fluctuation in the national and international prices on account of variable supply and demand that bring into conflict the interest of the growers and user industry. Growers are often exploited by middleman who force cleverly to part with their produce at much cheaper rates. There is need of fixation of pregrowing prices by the user industry for specific raw material to support the cultivation of medicinal plants. The buy back guarantee, assured by the user companies to the growers will encourage the cultivation of medicinal plants.

5. INEFFICIENT TRANSFER OF TECHNOLOGY

Quite a few technologies, agro technology, and improved varieties for a number of medicinal plants are available. These crops have not been covered by regular extension support in the country and therefore, many a time new cultures or improved technology has not reached the growers in a way expected for obtaining high yield.

SUGGESTIONS

1 Identification of potential zones for cultivation of Safed musli.

2 Identification and conservation of different species of Safed musli for commercial cultivation taking into consideration the demand and supply position.

3 Standardization of cultivation techniques for the identified species.

4 Ensuring availability of various inputs especially quality plant material and technical guidance to the cultivators.

5 Ensuring adequate processing, marketing and storage facilities.

6 Ensuring remunerative prices for the produce.

Processing of Safed Musli

It is a part of marketing service, which deals with the conversion of the produce into a more finished condition before it is offered for sale. Processing can be fully automated, semi-automatic or manual depending on the extent of cultivation. The processing of musli involves the following steps.

WASHING / CLEANING OF TUBERS

The dug out tubers from the soil, naturally contains lot of mud. So, the tubers are washed properly and disinfected. The healthier fingers are detached from the crown for peeling off skin.

PEELING

Peeling is a skilful operation and needs care and experience. It is nothing but removal of skin from the tubers.

- Select the tubers, which are not suitable for replanting (without crown) for peeling process.
- Peeling makes the tuber to dry easily
- Peeling with the special knife is most useful, one person can peel to the tune of 5 kg per day. Research is on for a faster way of peeling through chemical or by machinery.
- Skin should be removed with steel knives for good quality of dry safed musli

DRYING

- Peeled musli tubers can be dried for reducing the moisture content. This process will take about 7 days for complete drying
- The peeled fingers could be dried in green houses providing controlled sunlight to obtain better quality of dried musli.
- Peeled safed musli tubers (fingers) should be cleaned by washing with water and dried in the shade or sun by spreading in thin layers on white cloth. During this period the climate should be cloudless.

GRADING

The fully dried fingers of safed musli can be sorted in 'A', 'B' and 'C' grades on the basis of its colour and size.

PACKING

After drying of safed musli it is to be packed in airtight polybags to prevent entry of moisture.

WEIGHT LOSS

From the stage of harvest to till it goes for packing there is natural weight loss of musli. Shorter and stoughter the tuber, lesser would be the weight loss.

MARKETING

Against the back drop of huge domestic and international demand for dry musli and the fact that the gap between its demand and supply is gulf-wide, there is a ready demand for it.

Generally, the private commercial farms in Maharashtra, Andhra Pradesh, Chhattisgarh and Madhya Pradesh that supply the planting material themselves undertake to by back the processed musli at very remunerative prices. Besides, there are various pharmacy units as well as private traders who keep on scouting about to locate the farmers to procure the musli at farm gates. As such, marketing is fully assured.

Economics of Safed Musli

The total cost of production of Safed musli has been worked out to Rs. 2.9 lakh per acre, where the major component is the cost of the planting material of 6 quintals @ Rs. 400/ kg. As against this, the total income worked out to be Rs. 5lakhs which comprises the safe price of 4 quintals of dried musli @ Rs. 1000$ per kg and gains in the form of planting materials weighing 2.5 quintals. Accordingly, the net profit per acre, worked out to be Rs. 2.10 lakh. Probably no other crop offers within 8 to 9 months.

TAX AND SUBSIDY BENEFITS

Being a medicinal plant coming under horticultural crops, Musli cultivation entitles one to tax-free returns, under the scheme of "Development of Commercial Horticulture through production and post harvest management" of National Horticulture Board (NHB), back-ended capital investment subsidy @ 20%, subject to a maximum limit of Rs. 25 lakh is available. Financial support from banks is available for the cultivation of musli. The availability of Safed musli has been steadily declining due to over exploitation and depleting forest cover. Government of India has declared it as endangered species seven years back. To encourage cultivation of Safed musli, National Medicinal Plant Board is offering a subsidy of 30% on the project cost. The National Horticultural Board is also offering incentives to encourage cultivation of this plant. To attract more entrepreneurs to take up musli cultivation, GOI has exempted the income from income tax.

In order to position the medicinal plants sector on its growth path and to preserve the rich plant resources through insitu conservation and to promote the cultivation of medicinal plants on a sustainable basis through peoples participation, GOI has set up a national level body known as "National Medicinal Plant Board" under the ministry of Health and Family Welfare, NABARD has identified medicinal plants as "Thrust Area" and decided to provide 100% refinance to eligible institutions at a concessional rate of 6.5% per annum for loans upto Rs. 25, 000 and 6.75 per annum for any loan above Rs. 25, 000. This will enable the banks to keep a reasonable margin and also offer lower rate of interest to the farmers of medicinal plant.

Incidentally, one Agri Export Zone (AEZ) exclusively for medicinal crops has been notified in Uttaranachal and some more in the pipeline. NABARD has also decided to conduct a few sensitization programmes for official institutions to be conducted by reputed institutions / universities dealing with medicinal plants in association with the National Plant Board.

Market Demand of Safed Musli

The recent times have been a witness to the resurgence of medicinal plants in human healthcare. The spiraling popularity of plant derived healthcare products can be traced to the advent of "green health boom" across the world. Apart from its gradually growing use in pharmaceutical, phytopharmaceutical and nutraceutical companies, medicinal plants are finding increasing use as raw material in diverse industries like cosmetics, detergents, dyes, insecticides and paints etc. By virtue of being the home of Ayurveda, India has naturally been a huge market for safed musli. In addition, increasing awareness and appreciation of the "natural goodness" of herbal products across the world has blostered the demand for Safed musli. Many countries in the Gulf, Europe and USA have traditionally been the major importers of the dry roots of safed musli for its use in the making of an assorted range of herbal products. At present, according to an estimate the world requirement of Safed musli is 35,000 tonnes per annum but current production is 5000 tonnes only. As a protein rich food supplement, there is a tremendous growth in international demand for processed Safed musli.

There is no-gainsaying the fact that Safed musi is an inevitable ingredient in any immunity-strengthening drugs. By virtue of being the home of Ayurveda, India as naturally been a huge market for Safed musli. Also in Western India, especially in Gujarat, people are given to the habit of taking a spoon of Safed musli along with milk twice a day as a part of routine healthcare. The roots of musli are widely used as a natural "sex tonic" and is an integral part of more than 100 herbal drug formulations. There are also instances of Safed musli being used in various ways in varied parts of the country.

Although, Indian forests are rich in Safed musli demand is increasing rapidly in Indian and international drug markets. This has created a pressure on Indian forests and if steps for timely conservation are not taken, the Indian forest will loss this valuable plant.

Of late, Pfizer's Viagra has been a sensation all over the world for its aphrodisiac qualities. It has proved to highly useful for people suffering from erectile dysfunction. But, as the drug has a chemical base, it has many potential side effects. It is reported to have serious effects on nerves and grave repercussions for cardiac patients on the contrary, Safed musli is a safe and effective drug with similar benefits and without any side effects. Alive to it, the Gujarat State Forest Development Corporation launched a potency drug by name "**NAI CHETNA**" that has been enjoying widespread and increasing acceptance as an alternative to Viagra.

The largest global markets of Safed musli are China, France, German, Italy, Japan, Spain, UK and USA. Japan has the highest per capita consumption of botanical medicines in the world. In the US and Europe, the trade has typically been growing at an average of 10 per cent per annum because of the popularity of alternative treatments and increasing official recognition of the benefits herbal preparations. In 1997, the five top-selling species in the US were Echinacea, Garlic, Ginkgo, Golden seal and Saw palmetto. In 1999, the world market for herbal remedies was US \$ 19.4 billion, with Europe in the lead (US \$ 6.7 billion), followed by Asia (US \$ 5.1 billion), North America (US \$ 4.0 billion) Japan (US \$ 2.2 billion) and the rest of the world (US \$ 1.4 billion).

The market in China is large and shared between public and private ownership. Thirteen of the top companies producing Traditional Chinese Medicines (TCMS) are listed publicly on the domestic stock exchange.

China's total output of medicinal plants from both cultivated and wild-harvested source is 1.6 million tonnes. The total value of the finished TCM Sector in 1996 was US $ 3.7 billion. The estimate excludes domestic consumption, the inclusion of which would result in a far higher figure. Overall sales of botanical medicine products in China in 1995 were estimated at US $ 5 billion. The botanical medicine market in Japan in 1996 was estimated at US $ 2.4 billion.

Japan has the highest per capita consumption of botanical medicines in the world and sales have grown rapidly in recent years, mainly because doctors increasingly incorporate TMC as a complement to western medicinal.

India is a major export of raw medicinal plants and processed plant – based drugs. Exports of crude drugs from India in 1994-95 were valued at US $ 53,219 million. Among crude drugs important once are plantago ovata (Psyllium), Panar spp. (Gineng), Cassia spp (Senna) and Catharanthus roseus (Rosy periwinkle). Nearly 75 per cent of total exports from India are sent to six countries, viz., France, Germany, Japan, Switzerland, UK and United States. Other major importing countries are Bangladesh, Pakistan and Spain.

THE MARKET IN EUROPE

Europe is a major world trader in medicinal plants. Germany is the leading European importer, accounting for a one third of both the total volume and the total value of European imports with France, Italy, Spain and UK among the other 12 leading importing countries. The 12 leading exporting countries in

Europe are lead by Germany, Bulgaria and Poland among these Germany accounting for one fifth of the volume and one third of the value. Germany is the major European trader in medicinal plants being the pivotal country in intra-European trade and acting as a link between markets in Eastern and South Eastern Europe and those in the North and West. The German Phytomedical market grew at 30 per cent between 1993 and 1995 from a value of US $ 2.5 billion to US $ 3.26 billion. The estimated growth rate in 1998-99 was 5-10 per cent. Twenty one companies dominate the German market.

The UK is the fourth largest market in Europe. Britain lost direct access to suppliers in Eastern Europe after the fall of communism, the trade becoming directed to an even greater extent than previously through Germany. Activities are currently under way to re-establish and strengthen formers trade links between the UK and Easter Europe. Bulgaria is the most important source country for European medicinal plants with average net exports of 7,000 tonnes per annum. Sixty to seventy per cent of medicinal plants produced or harvested in Bulgaria are exported mainly to wholesalers in Germany. Bulgarcoop, a cooperative enterprise instituted under the communist regime, is still the main national dealer in medicinal plants, even in this post-communist era. This cooperative helps growers with cultivation and guarantees to by an agreed harvest. Since, the fall of communism 50-60 private and small companies, often family owned, have joined the medicinal plant trade and founded the Private Herb Exchange (PHE), which provides similar help to growers to Bulgarcoop and also organizes courses for collectors.

MEDICINAL PLANT TRADE STRUCTURE IN EUROPE

In Europe the trade structure is complex and dominated by a few wholesalers. In producer countries generally, various types of traders, including local dealers, village cooperatives and District traders, bring the plant material from collectors and cultivators. It is then passed on to wholesalers, manufactures or directly to retailers. The wide range of manufactures involved can include those engaged in the production of pharmaceuticals, Extracts, Cosmetics, Foods and colouring agents, material of a species which has entered the wholesale or manufacturing sectors may have originated from various harvesting areas within countries or it could even have been imported. This makes it very difficult to identify sources of materials and to impose quality controls. The lengths of trade chains and the perceived need to protect information lead to a lack o transparency. A direct consequence is that those at the start of the chains (producers and collectors) have little idea of the market value of the medicinal plants which they are supplying, not the means of discover the value added from source to end-use.

In India and Nepal some NGO's are working to make market information available to collectors in order to give them more bargaining power. The lack of transparency means that it is difficult to influence the trade easily in order to improve the sustainability of the source of medicinal plants.

In former Eastern Block Countries, the trade has changed in recent years from strictly organized, state-controlled systems based mostly on country-wide networks, to free and diversified markets with an increasing number of competing private companies. This has had significant negative effects on the sustainability and conservation of medicinal plants because previous quotas and control are now largely ignored. Only Bulgaria still has a relatively well controlled medicinal plant trade.

Future Thrust Areas in Safed Musli

India is among the few countries gifted with the unique geographical features that are essential for cultivation of an array of rare medicinal plants with rich commercial potential. Yet, the country has not realized and reaped the full potential of such plants through scientific farming. It is clear that organized and scientific cultivation of Safed musli is necessitated by increasing demand supply gap.

SEGREGATION OF PLANT VARIETIES

Classification of the plant varieties, based on the differences in physical properties and the resultant impact on tuber growth.

IRRIGATION TECHNOLOGIES

Identification of appropriate irrigation technologies vis-à-vis diverse soils, based on moisture requirement and retention analysis.

MULCHING TECHNOLOGIES

Identification of appropriate mulching techniques for reduced weeding, improved moisture retention and optimal growth of tubers.

ORGANIC FARMING

Production of "natural" and "quality" product in line with the requirement of international market by leveraging latest breakthroughs in biotechnology.

STORAGE PRACTICES

Developing suitable storage practices to guard the tubers against pests, decay and loss of moisture and thereby improve their shelf life.

HRVESTING PRACTICES

Evolving effective and efficient ways of harvesting to avoid possible damage or loss of tubers in the process.

PROCESSING PRACTICES

Innovating cost-effective processing techniques for extraction of saponins from the tubers to ensure utmost purity and quality.

- Conservation of available genotypes and mass multiplication using biotechnology and conventional approaches.
- Documentations of herbal plants with their validity
- Standardization of agrotechniques Safed musli
- Modern extraction procedure and packaging of Musli formulations with their pharmacognocy
- Training the farmers about cultivation and processing of Musli tubers
- Collection of old literature like palm script and by using the procedure available in them for preparation of formulations

- Government has to fix some market value of Musli products based on quality at procurement centres and in regulated markets.
- Solicitation of cooperation between National Medicinal Plant Board with relevant state government agencies.

Questions and Answers

Q1. Can we save Chlorophytum in Indian forests?

Due to the heavy demand of different useful parts of valuable plants, their availability is continuously decreasing. Safed musli (*Chlorophytum borivilianum*) is among these plants. In Indian systems of medicine, Safed musli holds a reputed position. The Medicinal Plant Board has recognized Safed musli as the sixth important herb to be protected and promoted. It is widely used as natural sex tonic. This is the reason that it is an integral part of more than 100 Ayurvedic formulations used as sex tonic. Indian forests are rich in Safed musli. The survey conducted has revealed that due to its unique medicinal properties, its demand is increasing and has created a pressure on Indian forests, if steps for timely conservation will not be taken, the Indian forest will lost this valuable plant.

Q2. Are two crops of Safed musli possible in a year?

The Indian farmers and researchers are in search of methods through which the dormancy of Safed musli can be broken. At present, a single crop of Safed musli is possible in one year. The planting of Safed musli starts in June (at some places in May) and within four months it completes its life cycle. After completion of life cycle, the tubers of Safed musli remains inside the soil in dormant condition and next year when favourable conditions occur in May-June, it sprouts again.

As its duration is only four months, three crops of Safed musli are possible, if we ignore the problem of dormancy for sometimes, two crops in a year can be taken easily in this case. Till now very less researches conducted on this aspect.

Q3. Is the income from cultivating Safed musli taxable?

Musli cultivation comes under agricultural income which is completely exempted from income tax under section 1-A of the Indian income-tax Act 1961.

Q4. Do banks provide finance for cultivating Safed musli?

Yes, most of the banks in India are today providing loans for medicinal plants cultivation, including Safed musli.

Q5. What is the consultancy fees charged by the private farms?

Consultancy fees charged by the private farms in two parts i.e. registration fee and final fee. The registration fee Rs. 5,000 per acre has to be paid at the start of the project and final fee of Rs. 15,000 per acre to be paid after the harvest when you receive the income from the selling of Safed musli. This will vary with the farms.

Q6. When is the planting season for Safed musli?

Safed musli is planted just after the monsoon rains during June-July period.

Q7. If the land lies in altitude of 200 meters to 2000 meters and soil pH of 5 is it possible to grow Safed musli?

Safed musli is reported to occur to a height of 1000 meters. The experiment has to be taken for cultivating Musli at higher altitudes for better growth. The soil pH should be around 6.5-7.5. Generally, it needs soils with good drainage system i.e. red sandy loams soils are ideal for its cultivation.

Q8. Why there is so much demand for Safed musli?

The increasing popularity of plant derived healthcare products can be attributed to the advent of green health boom across the world. Because their gradually growing use in pharmaceuticals, phytopharmaceutical and neutraceutical companies, medicinal plants are finding increasing use as raw material in diverse industries cosmetics, detergents, dyes, insecticides, paints etc. Safed musli is among the 20 natural medicinal plants that is finding increasing appreciation and application in the market of health boosters, body toners and health rejuvenators. Globally demand for Safed musli is estimated at 35,000 tons per annum, whereas the quantum available is only 5000 tons. Even of the 5,000 tons available, 98% of produce mainly comes from wild harvesting.

Q9. What are the technologies used for peeling and drying?

Peeling has to be done immediately after the harvest and special type of knives are used by women for peeling. Drying is a process wherein the peeled Safed musli tubers are kept under shade for 4-7 days, to lose moisture to the tune of 75-80%.

Q10. What is the minimum area required for profitable Safed musli plantation?

You can start cultivation of Safed musli with one acre and expand further in the coming years.

Q11. Does the government support Musli cultivation?

Having notified Safed musli as an endangered species, the government of India discourages collection of it from forest sources and provides various facilities and subsidies for mainstream cultivation of the medicinal plants. Besides, financial support for cultivation of Safed musli is also available on attractive terms from various financial institutions.

Q12. Where all Safed musli is being cultivated in India?

In view of its increasing demand and excellent returns on investment, Safed musli is increasingly coming under mainstream cultivation. The front liners among the states in Safed musli cultivation are Andhra Pradesh, Karnataka, Tamil Nadu and Chattisgarh.

Q13. Do you think the Safed musli can sustain present price in coming years?

In USA, one fourth of the 5 hundred million prescription written are reported to contain leaf plant extract (WHO). The demand in other countries is increasing, hence there would be a growing demand for Safed musli in the near future.

Important Website Address of Safed Musli Exproters

- www.123india.com
- www.geocities.com/gouravmuslifarm
- www.indiamart.com
- www.indiamart.com/greenagribiotech
- www.indiamart.com/mulltiherbal
- www.indiamart.com/rajasthanherbal
- www.jeevanherbs.com
- www.krdmuslifarm.com
- www.maaumiyasafedmuslifarm.com
- www.motherherbs.com
- www.nandanagrofarms.com
- www.nandanmusli.com
- www.rajchamber.com
- www.safedmusli.net
- www.safedmusli.ref
- www.safedmuslicapitalofindia.com
- www.saurabhfarm.com
- www.shivammusli.com

List of Safed Musli Growers on India

1. APFDC (ANDHRA PRADESH FOREST DEVELOPMENT CORPORATION)

The APFDC has taken up the cultivation of this prestigious herb from 2001-2002 onwards in Eastern Ghats (Rajahmundry), Nallamalais (Kurnool District) and Rang Reedy District. Cultivation is done most scientifically following totally on organic farming to enhance the quality of the active ingredients available in it. The APEDC is cultivating Safed musli by organic farming 17 acres of land and it has been decided to sell the planting material to prospective growers of Safed musli at a reasonable rate to promote the species. The rate is Rs. 250 / kg of wet planting material at site.

Contact address

Vice-Chairman and Managing Director,
AP Forest Development Corporation Ltd,
3rd Floor, UNI Building, A.C. Guards,
Hyderabad – 500 004.
Phone: 191-40-23392652, Fax: +91-40-23320032
E-mail: ve&md_apfdc@ap.gor.in
dm_m_apfdc@rediffmail.com

2. ACEAGRO FOODS PVT. LTD.,

It is one of the premier organization involved in the production and export of Safed musli produce.

Facilities

- They will provide disease free Safed musli planting material.
- **Technical support**: They will guide in land preparation/setting up of the drip system/planting/use of nutrients and compost/weeding and crop protection/ harvesting /peeling and packing practices.

Support products

It provides the necessary bio-compost and bio-fertilizers specially prepared for this plant.

Marketing support

They will provide market for the product.

Contact address

ACEAGRO,
VIII, Kondivade, Post Takare Budruk,
Tal.Mawal, Dt. Pune,
Pune – 412 106, Maharashtra (India),
Ph: +91-2114-244244
E-mail: indiaroses@aceagro.com
deepan@aceagro.com

3. SAURABH FARMS LIMITED

They are the main producers and exporters of Safed musli tubers. Their total production is mainly goes for international market.

E-mail: info@saurabhafarms.com.

4. MAA DANTESHWARI HERBAL FARMS

- This farm is located at Chattisgarh.
- They provide free training at farm itself.
- They also provide all kinds of technical know-how support and backup to all those who want to do business with them.

E-mail: training@safedmusi.info.

5. KRD MUSLI FARM

KRD Musli farm is a famous and developed farm of Indore (MP). This farm is the producer of quality Safed musli planting material by using high-tech agriculture techniques.

Features and facilities

- They provide consultancy and training for cultivating Safed musli and free services to those persons who are interested in undertaking experiments and research in the field of cultivation or processing of Musli.
- Best quality planting material
- Advance agriculture technique
- Provide market related information
- Advance booking facilities
- Expert storage techniques
- Consultancy on cultivation technique with free of cost
- Quick and online information via website and e-mail.

6. MOTHER HERBS

Head office

Mother herbs
1, Deen Dayal Radhey Shyam,
Mangal Padav, Haldawani – 263139.
Dist – Nanital (Uttaranchal)
Fax: 91-5946-252368.
E-mail: info@motherherbs.com

Marketing office

91802 East End Apartments,
Mayur Vihar, Phase 1 Extn.
New Delhi – 110096. (India).
Ph: +91-(11)-33424338.

7. MITTAL MUSLI FARM

It is Maharashtra based Safed musli farm provides farmers and corporate houses with high quality planting material, consultancy to grow the crop as well as a buyback guarantee. They also provide free training for the cultivation of Safed musli.

8. JEEVAN HERBS AND AGRO FARMS

This farm involved in the cultivation and trade of musli. They supply planting material as well as provide consulting services to the corporate and individual farmers.

Contact address

Jeevan herbs and agro farms,
178, Keshav Ganj,

Sagar (MP) – 470 002, India.
Tel: +91-7582-233049; Fax:+91-7582-233859
E-mail: staip@sancharnet.in.sales@jeevanherbs.com
mouterplaza@vsnl.com

Marketing office

B-39, Vivek Vihar,
Phase- 1, Delhi – 110 095
India, Tel: +91-11-22153319.

9. SAUBHAGYA KALPATARU PVT LTD.,

It is located at Hinganghat in Maharashtra and produces tissue culture Safed musli medicianl plants.

10. SHIVAM MUSLI FARM

11. MAA UMIYA SAFED MUSLI FARM

This farm is located at Malwa, which is situated in west of Madhya Pradesh. They supply quality planting material of Safed musli.

12. NANDAN AGRO FARMS PVT. LTD.,

It is situated in Hyderabad. It provides the necessary inputs and technical support. Nandan's Safed musli resource centre is well equipped to impart training, scientific cultivation and crop management methodologies of Safed musli.

The resource centre conducts infield short duration training modules involving practice oriented approach by experts in medicinal plants. Further, the trainees are provided with manuals and other supplementary literature to guide them through the implementation of the project from land preparation up to post-harvest phase.

List of Indian Companies Purchasing Medicinal Plants

1 **Aditya Alkaloids Ltd.,**
8-2-6555/2/2, Somajiguda,
Hyderabad – 500 482.
Ph: 210396/210430

2 **Almighty Exports**
4, Nehru Street, Alwarthiru Nagar,
Valasaravakkam,
Chennai – 600 087.
Ph: 423536, Fax: 044-4831793

3 **American Remedies**
124, LB Road, PB No. 928,
Adayar, Chennai -600 020.
Ph: 412599,
Fax: 91-44-415902

4 **Anthyodhaya Sangh**
Ethno Medicinal Plants Conservation,
Viduthalaipuram,
Lalgudi-Padalur Road,
Tiruchi, Ph: 760443 Fax: 760063.

5 **Arya Vaidya Nilayam**
P.B. No. 4, 175-A, Muniandipuram, (P.O) Pasumalai,
Madurai – 625 004. Ph: 0452-771593

6 **Astanga Arya Vaidya Sale**
5, Chinnakkadai St.,
Trichy -2. Ph: 0431-701074.

7 **Ayurchem Products**
31/32, Patil Bhauvan,
Netaji Subash Road,
Mulund, Mumbai – 400 080.
Ph: 5603285

8 **Baidyanath Ayurved Bhavan Ltd.,**
21-7-802 Opp. High Court,
Hyderabad -500 002.
Ph: 522068

9 **Balaj Sevashram Ltd.,**
17-1204/8, Saidabad,
Hyderabad – 500 659
Ph: 528768

10 **Balamukund Devkaran Sharda**
15-7-320 Devkripa, Begum Bazar,
Hyderabad – 500 002.
Ph: 552425, 45016.

11 **Bcerhringr – Knocil Ltd.,**
Kolshet Road,
Thana, Mumbai – 400 607.

12 **Bharat Pharma**
3/9, Sakchi, P.B. No. 21
Jamshedpur – 831 001

13 **Bharat Pharma**
3/9, Sakchi, P.O. No. 21,
Jamshedpur – 831 001.

14 **Bismilla Exporters**
95, Veverpuram Road,
Tuticorin – 628 003.

15 **Cadila Pharmaceuticals Ltd.,**
IRM House, Office Road,
Navrangapura,
Ahmedabad – 380 009.
(Gujarat)

16 **Charak Pharmaceuticals (India) Ltd.,**
Ever green Industrial Estate
Shakti Mills Lane,
Dr. E. Moses Road,
Mahalaxmi,
Mumbai-400011 M.H.

17 **CIPLA Ltd.,**
Virgenagar, P.O.
Bangalore – 560 049.

18 **Continental Traders**
5, Cunnigham Crescent,
Post Box. 108,
Bangalore – 560 062.

19 **Dabur India Ltd.,**
3-9, 1107, Anand Towers,
Gunfoundry,
Hyderabad- 500 001.
Ph: 241482

20 **Dabur India Ltd.,**
8/3, Asaf Ali Road,
Darya Ganj,
New Delhi – 110002.

21 **Dabur Pvt. Ltd.**
8/3, Asaf Ali Road,
New Delhi – 110 002.

22 **Dabur Pvt. Ltd.,**
8/3, Asaf Ali Road,
New Delhi – 110 002.

23 **Dabur Research Foundation**
8/3, Asaf Ali Road,
New Delhi – 110 002.
Ph: 3271001, 3276739.

24 **Dhoot Papershwar Ltd.,**
135, Nanubhai Desai Road,
Opp. Wilson High School,
Mumbai – 400004.
Maharashtra

25 **Foundation for Revitalization of Local Health & Traditions**
50, MSH Lay Out, 2nd Stage,
3rd Main, Anand Nagar,
Bangalore – 560 024.
Ph: 3336909 Fax: 3334167

26 **Government Herbarium & Ayurvedic Factory**
Sivarampally Kattedam,
Industrial Area, Hyderabad.

27 **Gujarat Ayurved Vikas Mandal Grishmakunj,**
Nr. Jcshipura Rly Crossing,
Junagadh – 362 002. Ph: 20042.

28 **Hankeem Chinoni Pharmacy**
Hakeem Chicni Street,
Romi Talac,
Surat – 395 002, Gujarat

29 **Hari Ram & Sons,**
412, Katra Maidgaran,

Khari baoli,
New Delhi – 110006.

30 **Herba Indica**
351, Industrial Area – II
Chandigarh – 160 002
Ph: 536729.

31 **Indfrag Pvt. Ltd.**
S-913, Manipal Centre,
Dickenson Road,
Bangalore – 560 042.

32 **Indian Drugs & Botanical Herbs Company Ltd.**
103, Ram Nagar, P.B. No. 9416,
Krishna Nagar,
Delhi- 110 051. Ph: 2415898

33 Indian Herbs,
P.B.No. 5,
Shardanagar,
Saharanpur -247001.
Uttar Pradesh.

34 **Indo German Alkaloids**
GA Building – Inga Complex
Andheri Eat
Mumbai – 400 093.
Ph: 0091-22-8342932
Fax: 0091-22-8364049

35 **Indo World Trading Corporation**
303, Prakash Chambers,
6, Netaji Subash Marg,
Darya Ganj,
New Delhi – 110 002.

Ph: 3278059
Fax: 91-11-3274521

36 **Indo-World Trading Corporation**
48, Parda Bagh, Darya Gunj
New Delhi – 110 002 Ph: 3278059.

37 **INFAR (India) Ltd.,**
7, Wood Street,
Calcutta – 700 016.

38 **IPSJ Neptune Overseas Corporation**
GPO Box. 554, Mumbai – 400 001

39 **J.J. Dechane Laboratories Pvt. Ltd.,**
4-1-326, Troop Bazar,
Hydeerabad – 500 001.

40 **Jenson Enterprises**
P.O. Bag No. 905,
34, New Thandavaraya Street,
Chennai. Ph: 551942.

41 **K. Fazlullah Khan**
Asian Orchards,
AC 52, TV Street, Anna Nagar,
Chennai – 600 040.

42 **Krishna Gopal Ayurved Bhawan,**
Mehra Building,
Jaipur Road,
Ajmer – 305 001.
Rajasthan.

43 **Madan Mchan Chem-med**
702/19, Padma Nagar,
University Road,
Hyderabad – 500 044.

44 **Maharishi Ayurved Products**
17-18, Noida Exports,
Processing Zone,
Noida – 201305, U.P.

45 **Manuel International**
39, Pedariar Koil Street,
Chennai – 600 001.

46 **Maxo Laboratories Pvt. Ltd.,**
115-A, Kamla Nagar,
New Delhi – 110 007.

47 **Mysore Essential Oils and Naturals**
No. 11, 2nd Cross, 5th Main,
Ganganhalli Extension,
Bangalore – 560 032.
Ph: 3333621

48 **N. Shobha Kant & Company**
59, Govindappa Nayakan Street, Chennai – 600 001.

49 **National Pharma**
Medical College Road,
Thanjavur – 613 009
Ph: 04362/40179

50 **Natural Remedies (P) Ltd.,**
Mahananda Arch,
No. 242/29, 2nd Floor,
9th Main,
Jaya Nagar, 3rd Block,
Bangalore (Karnataka).

51 **Orient Pharma Pvt. Ltd.,**
Old Trunk Road,
Pallavaram, Madras – 600 043.

52 **Roop Pharma,**
A-1, Udyo Nagar,
Navsari, Gujarat.

53 Sandu Brothers (P) Ltd.
D.K. Sandu Marg,
Chembur, Mumbai – 400071 M.H.

54 **Sapal & Company**
113, Caveri Street,
Mumbai – 400 002.

55 **Schokhi Industries Pvt. Ltd.,**
143, Jolly Marker,
14th Floor, 255, Nariman Point,
Mumbai- 400 021.

56 **Shahnz Husains Herbal**
17/1-A,
Madan Mohan Malviya Marg,
Lucknow – 226 001.
Ph: 0522-282813

57 **Shree Baidhyanth,**
Ayurveda Bhawan
Baidhyantha Bhawan Road,
Patna – 800 001.

58 Shree Baidyanath Ayurved Bhawan Ltd.
1, Gupta Lane,
Kolkata – 700006, W.B.

59 **Shree Baidyanath Ayurved Bhawan Ltd.,**
172, Gusainpura,
Jhansi-284002 U.P.

60 **Shree Baidyanath Ayurved Bhawan Ltd.,**
Naini, Allahabad – 211008,
Uttar Pradesh.

61 **Southern Herbals Ltd.,**
45, Ramraj Mansion,
100 Ft Road, Vysya Bank Colony, BTM, II Stage,
Bangalore – 560 076.

62 **SUR Pharmaceuticals**
3, Bharat Building
Irla Soceity Road,
Vile Parie (West),
Bombay – 400 056.

63 **SVR Pharmaceuticals**
3, Bharat Building,
Irla Society Road,
Virle Parle (West),
Mumbai – 400 056.

64 **Tamil Nadu Medicinal Plants Corp. Ltd.,**
Anna Hospital Campus, Arumbakkam,
Chennai – 600 106.

65 **Trichy Ayurvedic Union (P) Ltd.,**
31-A, Chinnakadai St., Trichy – 620 002.
Ph: 0431-704202.

66 **Vijay Laboratories**
E-1, Industrial Estate,
Talkatora, Lucknow – 226 011 (U.P)

67 **Wayeth Laboratories Ltd.,**
3006, HAL II stage,
Bennarghatta Road,
Bangalore – 560 076 Ph: 5583567

68 **West Coast Home Products Pvt. Ltd.**
P.B. No. 6897
58, Hosur Main Road, Near Madiwala Post,
Bangalore – 560 068
Ph: 5534814, Fax: 080-5533022.

List of Foreign Companies Purchasing Medicinal Plants

1 **Aphrodisia Products Inc.**
45, Washington St.,
Brooklyn, Ny 11201,
New York (212)-852-1278, USA.

2 **World Herb Co. Inc**
459-18th Ave,
New York 3 (New Jersey),USA.

3 **Aloe Laboratories Texas**
RT. 1 Box 161
Lyford, Texas, 78569, USA

4 **BCR Natural Extract Processing Co. Inc.**
62 N. Industry Street, Deer Park,
NY 11729 (516) 242-4020
New York, USA.

5 **Botanicals International Inc.**
2550 EI Presidio Street,
Long Beach,
CA 90810 (2130 637-9566)
California, USA.

6 **Burlington Bio-Medical Corp.**
100, Fairchil.Av., Plainview,
NY 11803 (516) 349-8800,
New York, USA.

7 **Charabot & Co. Inc.**
83, Cedar Lane, Englewood NJ
07631 (201) 569-8585
New Jersey, USA.

8 **Chart Corp.**
519, Broad Street, Glen Roack,
NJ 07452 (201) 445-5556,
New Jersey, USA.

9 **Cominso (Canada) Ltd.**
351, Place Royale,
Montreal, Canada.

10 **Sluys International NV**
Heuvelstrat 3-2530,
Boechout, Belgium,
Ph: (03) 4552255, Fax (03) 455 1693.

11 **Natures Herb Company**
345 O' Farrell Street,
San Fransisco 2 (Calif) USA,

12 **Dominion Herb Distributors Inc.,**
1447-51, St. Laurance,
Boulevard, Montreal Canada.

Important Drugs of Safed Musli and their Manufactures

Drugs	Manufactures
Aarogya Chywanprash	**Aarogya Herbals Pvt. Ltd.,** A-6/7, Vasant Vihar, 2nd Floor, New Delhi- 110 057, India. Ph: 91-11-26147287; Fax: 91-11-26147287 www.indiamart.com/aarogyaherbals.
Bahar	**Himalaya Chemical Laboratory Pharmacy** (Regd.) 31, 4B Block, Koramangala, Bangalore – 560 034, India. Ph: 91-80-25534392; Fax: 91-80-25534392 www: indiamart.com/himalaya
Chawanprash	**Saimax Exports Pvt. Ltd.,** 108, Creative Industrial Estate, Sundar Nagar, Mumbai – 400 098, India. www.indiamart.com/selmaxexports.
Chyawanprash	**Devicas Herbal Pvt. Ltd.,** E-1/70, Areracolony, Bhopal, - 462 016, India. Ph: 91-755-2464702; Fax: 91-755-5284020 www.indiamart.com/devicaasherbal
Dabur Chayawanprash	**Dabur Pvt. Ltd.**
e-lix-r	**Elixir Tonics and Teas** California, USA.
Endurx	**Nutrilabs Intenrational, Inc.** USA, Ph: 1-415-863-2363 Fax: 1-415-707-2122
Geriforte. Geriforteaqua Geriforte vet	**Himalaya herbal health group**

Drugs	Manufactures
Herbal sexual vitalizer	**Saimusli** ≠ 8221, C/o Tourist Resort, Tourist Complex, Nehru Chowk, ≠ 8211, Station Road, Jalgaon – 425 001, Maharashtra, India. E-mail: Saimusli@yahoo.com Saimusli @rediffmail.com
La-Tone Gold Capsules Lecuwell Capsules La – Tone	**La-medicca (India) Pvt. Ltd.** 434, Udyog Vihar, Phase III, Dundahera, Gurgaon – 122 016. www.indiamart.com/la-medica/index.html.
Nai chetna (Sex tonic)	**Gujarat Forest development Corporation** (GFDc)
Taprodis	**Trimph's herbal Ltd.,**
Vega Asia Sex tablet Vega Power Capsules Vega Gold Capsules Viagra Cialis Levitra Vega – plus capsules Vega – EX Vega – K2 capsules	**Vee Excel Drugs and Pharmaceuticals Pvt. Ltd.,** G-16, Preet Vihar, Vikas Marg, New Delhi – 110 092, India. Ph: 91-11-22058687 Fax: +(91)-(11)-22044647 www.vxldrugs.com.
Vigor & Vitality Capsules	**Amazing Herbal Remedies** A 75, South Extension 1, New Delhi – 110 049, India. Fax: +91-11-51646221 www.indiamart.com/amazingherbalremedies.
Vimax – 500	**Healthmax pharama** 320, Vardhaman City Centre, Near Shakthi Nagar Flgover, New Delhi – 110 052, India. Ph: 91-11-23645516 www.indiamart.com/healthmaxpharma
Vita-Ex Gold Kamini Vindravan Ras Baidyanath muslipak	**Baidyanata Ayurved Bhavan Ltd.,** 21-7-802 Opp. High Court, Hyderabad – 500 002. Ph: 522068

Quality Evaluation of Herbal Drugs

In India, the single most important factor that is standing in the way of wider acceptance of drugs based on medicinal plants is non-availability or inadequacy of standard to check or test the quality by modern instrumentation methods. A serious thought needs to be given to this aspect. Even with the best of intentions, no system of medicine can achieve any degree of creditability and mass acceptance unless some degree of quality control or quality assurance is maintained. In fact, this lack of regulation governing the identification and quality of herbs in the international trade has enabled substitutes, adulterated as well as fake plants to penetrate the international market, thus giving a bad name to the particular system of medicine.

There are 5 steps to ensure the quality evaluation and standardization of herbal drugs:

1 **Organoleptic parameters-** It includes colour, odour, taste, texture and fracture.

2 **Botanical parameters-** It includes microscopic as well as macroscopic analysis. Microscopic analysis includes Qualitative, Quantitative and Powder studies. Macroscopic analysis includes Shape and External marking.

3 **Physical parameters-** It includes moisture content, extractive values, ash values and fluorescence Analysis.

4 **Chemical parameters-** It includes Qualitative and Quantitative (HPTLC, finger printing, Secondary Metabolites, DNA finger printing), Chromatography (HPTLC, GLC, HPLC), heavy metals, pesticide residue and Mycotoxin.

5 **Biological parameters-** It includes microbial contamination, Toxicological, Pharmacological, antagonistic (Bacterial, Fungal) and other specific activities.

BENEFITS OF QUALITY EVALUATION

1 Importance and acceptability of indigenous system of medicine increases many folds.

2 Quality assurance

3 Batch to batch consistency

4 Increased export potential

5 Desired therapeutic effects

6 Foreign strong linkage between pharmaceutical industries and national labs.

Role of Global Safed Musli Foundation (GSMF)

GSMF is aimed at promoting and encouraging the herbal industry with scientific reference to Safed musli plant. The foundation targets all the segments of Cultivation, Processing, Product Manufacturing and Export of the plant. The foundation is committed to the advancement of Scientific and Systematized method of Cultivation on one hand and strives to develop value addition of the therapeutic properties of the plant on the other hand.

The foundation is common trading platform for all the existing Growers, Prospective Entrepreneurs, Traders, Commission agents and Exporters. The foundation encourages all the Scientists and Researchers to probe the plant of its inherent values

ACTIVITIES

- The foundation is primarily to assist in helping enlist members, promote and coordinate programs through the **GSMF** office in **Hyderabad** (India).
- Its governing body that its founder members will carry on administrative activities of **GSMF** permanently.
- The common bond between this diverse group of individuals i.e. governing body and associate members is an interest in promoting **Safed Musli** and its use in medicinal products,

beverages, pharmaceuticals and a wide variety of other products.

- The foundation will open its branches in all prospective cities such as Chandigarh, Ahmadabad, Bangalore, Mumbai and other places like Mahu in Madhya Pradesh and in any other place or places that the governing body decides from time to time
- It is the endeavor of the foundation to create a common trading platform for the existing growers and the prospective entrepreneurs in **Safed musli** industry.
- The foundation will also stretch its full-fledged efforts to explore international and global market and also for value addition program of **Safed musli** dry material as well as products.
- The foundation will assist its associate members in marketing their produce.
- The foundation shall undertake sales promotion activities of seed material as well as dried material of **Safed Musli** through its websites and through other publication media and also by participation in various Agri-Exhibitions, Trade Fares and Seminars.
- The entire expenditure for its promotional activities, Research and development activities and also to meet administrative expenses, **GSMF** will pool up funds from possible resources.
- The governing body shall be the sole deciding authority in all aspects such as price fixation and in relation to other activities of the foundation.
- **GSMF** serves as a liaison and information source for development, promotion and research of **Safed Musli** in respect of cultivation and associated products. All members,

associate members or subscribers with **GSMF** will have access to a wide variety of information, support and advice.

- **GSMF** will review trade publications and reports periodically on all **Safed Musli** industry news affecting business. When the industry news is urgent, the members receive emergency bulletins or press releases on the particular issue involved.
- **GSMF**, Membership gives the associate company constant access to other members, associate members and subscribers through **GSMF**'s publications.
- **GSMF** intends to evolve programs for proper gradation of raw materials and finished goods to assure people of using the purest, most beneficial **Safed Musli** possible. This program protects people and the industry from companies using adulterated **Safed Musli** and from making false product claims.
- **GSMF** intends to provide its members with references, pamphlets and manuals on regulations, technical advice, insurance protection possibilities, good manufacturing practices, environmental impact and other significant areas.
- **GSMF** present open board meetings once in a year where subjects of general interest are discussed. Every member, associate member and subscriber is invited.
- **GSMF** have an ongoing liaison with other trade associates and work with them to provide a united front on all matters of common interest
- **GSMF** is **CARE TAKER**. Its constant vigilance enables us to react instantly and challenge any legislation, regulation or adverse publicity that threatens the **Safed Musli** industry.
- Use every opportunity to improve public understanding of the role **GSMF** plays in representing the needs and concerns of the entrepreneur in the **Safed Musli** industry.

- **GSMF** work with regulatory bodies. It interacts with **Safed Musli** researchers.
- The foundation will hold meetings as needed and supply information to a relatively new market.
- Routine questions and general communications should be sent to the **GSMF** office as always the home office will monitor the activities to not duplicate efforts, but to improve communication and assist in the growth of **Safed Musli** Industry
- One of the key functions of the **International Safed Musli Foundation (ISMF)** is encouraging research and development of **Safed Musli.**
- **GSMF** have numerous scientists, doctors and other researchers around the world constantly performing tests and conducting research on the properties and benefits of **Safed Musli**. These researchers often write articles on their findings and **GSMF** has access to them for its members

Role of NABARD in Promotion of Medicinal Plants

In view of the potentialities available and the demand for herbs and herbal products, considerable importance is being attached by **NABARD** to the promotion of herbal plant cultivation, processing and other related activities.

Some of the important policies and development initiatives taken by NABARD include the following-.

1. ASSISTANCE FROM RESEARCH & DEVELOPMENT FUND

- NABARD extends grant assistance from Research and Development fund to Agriculture universities and NGOs who have got facilities to carryout the research on standardization of package of practices of medicinal plants and commercialization of technologies for adoption at field level.

- Grant assistance is also given for organizing national / international level workshops seminars in the field of medicinal plants.

2. DEVELOPMENTAL ROLE

- NABARD has embarked on the estimation of potential available for cultivation of medicinal plants and preparation of potential linked credit plan.
- Fixation of unit cost / scale of finance for medicinal plants to enable the bankers to finance for the sector.
- Creating awareness among the concerned about the scope and potential for cultivation of medicinal plants on commercial basis by organizing national regional level workshops and seminars.

3. RECENT POLICY INITIATIVES

National Medicinal Plants Board has proposed "Credit Linked Subsidy Programme" for the promotion of medicinal plants sector. In this regard, NABARD proposes to discuss with Government of India to finalize the draft guidelines prepared by NABARD for successful implementation of the scheme.

4. OTHER POLICY INITIATIVES

NABARD Consultancy Services (NABCONS)

NABARD has a core staff of technical officers in various disciplines viz., Plantation and Horticulture, Minor Irrigation, Wasteland and Watershed development, Animal husbandry, Fisheries, micro finance etc., for doing the consultancy services. NABARD undertakes the work of project formulation (project preparation), conduct of evaluation studies, monitoring studies, preparation of feasibility report for hitech projects etc for a nominal fee.

Contract farming

The traditional farming practices are undergoing a change with contract farming taking root with firm arrangements for buyback and increased income to farmers. Recognizing the importance of contact farming refinance is extended to banks at concessional rate of interest. Currently the rate of interest on refinance for such projects is kept at 6.75% irrespective of bank loan amount.

Cofinancing

Cofinancing of projects of larger outlays with commercial banks, maximum to the extend of 50% of the project cost. NABARD has already entered into MOU with Central Bank of India, Dena Bank, UCO Bank, Corporation Banks etc., for cofinancing the projects with them.

Brief Packages for Commercial Medicinal Crops

ALOE

1.	Scientific Name	*Aloe vera*
2.	Vernacular Name	Tamil-Thazhai, Hindi-Gheekanvar, Kannada-Lolesara, Sanskrit-Kumari
3.	Family	Liliaceae
4.	Economic part	Leaves
5.	Active principle/Chemical constituents	Anthraglucoside (aloin) -4.5-2.5%, Rich in malic, teartaric acids
6.	Species	*Aloe barbadensis, Aloe foerox, Aloe chinensis, Aloe indica, Aloe peyrii*
7.	Distribution	India, West Indies, South Africa
8.	Uses	Both drug and cosmetic industry
9.	Soil and Climate	Sandy coastal to loamy soils with pH upto 8.5 and requires warm humid or dry climate
10.	Propagation	Root suckers or rhizome cuttings
11.	Planting material	5000 suckers/acre
12.	Spacing	60x30cm or 60x45cm
13.	Irrigation	Mostly grown under rainfed conditions
14.	Weeding	Two weedings in a year
15.	Pests and Disease	No serous pest and disease incidence
16.	Harvesting	Harvesting starts from 6-7 months after planting. Three harvest per year (upto five years)
17.	Duration	Perennial (pay back period five years)

18.	Yield/ha	2000 kg dried leaves (first year) + 3000kg (2nd to 5th year)
19.	Economics	Cost of cultivation/ha First year = Rs. 60,000 2nd to 5th year = Rs. 30, 000 Gross return / ha = Rs. 70, 000 Net return/ ha 1st year = Rs. 10,000 2nd to 5th year = Rs. 30,000
20.	Market	Domestic and International
21.	Market price	Domestic : Rs. 30-35/kg International : $ 3.5 / kg

COLEUS

1.	Scientific Name	*Coleus forskohlii*
2.	Vernacular Name	Pashan bhedi (sanskrit), Patharchur (Hindi), Makandiberu (Kannadam)
3.	Family	Lamiaceae
4.	Economic part	Root
5.	Active principle	Forskohlin (coleonol) – 0.1-0.8%
6.	Varieties	K8
7.	Distribution	India, Africa, Egypt, Brazil, Arabia, Pakistan
8.	Uses	Drug for hypertension, congestive heart failures etc.
9.	Soil and Climate	Red sandy loam soils (pH 5-5.7) with marginal fertility tropical climate is ideal
10.	Propagation	Stem cuttings and seeds
11.	Planting material	80,000 seedlings/ha
12.	Spacing	60x20 cm
13.	Manures and fertilizers	40 kg N, 60 kg P_2O_5 and 50 kg K_2O /ha
14.	Irrigation	Irrigation immediately after transplanting weekly irrigation is sufficient for good growth
15.	Weeding	Frequent weeding during early stage of

		crop growth is necessary
16.	Pests	Leaf eating caterpillar, Mealy bugs and root knot nematodes. Control: Spraying or drenching the roots with 0.1% methyl parathion. For nematodes carbofuron granules @ 20 kg ha^{-1}
17.	Disease	Bacterial wilt Control: Spraying and drenching the soil adjoining the affected plants with 0.2% captan solution
18.	Harvesting	Crop harvested at 135-150 days after planting
19.	Duration	150 – 180 days
20.	Yield/ha	20 tonnes
21.	Economics/ha	Cost of cultivation = Rs. 25, 000 Gross returns = Rs. 80, 000 Net income = Rs. 55, 000
22.	Market	Domestic and international
23.	Market price	Domestic = Rs. 40-45 / kg of Dried roots = Rs. 4/kg of Fresh roots International = $ 85/100 gm of for skholin
24.	Buyers	MGP Marketing centers, Salem,TN.

GLORY LILY

1.	Scientific Name	*Gloriosa superba*
2.	Vernacular Name	Visalya (Sanskrit), Karihari Languli (Hindi)
3.	Family	Liliaceae
4.	Economic part	Seeds and Rhizomes
5.	Active principle/Chemical constituents	Superbine and colchicine, Colchicine content in Seeds – 0.6-1% Rhizomes – 0.1-0.2%
6.	Species	*G. plantii, G. carsonii, G. lutea, G. latifolia, G. longifolia, G. simplex*

7.	Distribution	India, Africa, Asia, Sri Lanka, USA, Madagascar
8.	Uses	Against Gout, Piles, Rheumatism and promote polyploidy
9.	Soil and Climate	Deep fertile well drained loamy soils (pH 6-7) and prefers warm humid climate
10.	Propagation	Rhizomes (50-60 gm) and seeds (one year old seedlings)
11.	Planting material	37,000 rhizomes (2t) or seedlings per hectare area
12.	Spacing	60x45cm
13.	Manures fertilizers	Vermicompost 2 t/acre and Gypsum @ 1 ton/acre a fertilizer dose of 120:50:75 kg NPK/ha is required for good crop
14.	Irrigation	Frequent irrigation during sprouting with held irrigation after flowering to prevent rotting of tubers
15.	Weeding	Initial stages requires frequent weeding. Chemical weed control is possible under wider spacing between rows
16.	Support	Being a weak climber, it requires support through trellies or live fence
17.	Pests and Disease	Less serious pest and disease Diseases like leaf blight, tuber rot and wilting are common Control: Drenching the soil with bavistin @ 0.2% near root zone to control rot and wilt diseases
18.	Harvesting	The right time of harvest is when the capsules starts turning light-green from dark green and the skin of the fruit shows a sunken appearance and become light in weight
19.	Duration	170-180 days
20.	Yield and Economics	Seeds: 250-300 kg/ha Rhizomes: 2.5-3.0 t/ha (after five years) Cost of cultivation: Rest. 35, 000 Gross return: Rs. 62, 000 Net return: Rs. 27, 000

21.	Market	Domestic and international
22	Price	Seeds: Rs. 250 / kg;Rhizomes: Rs.30 / kg (Domestic)

KALMEGH

1.	Scientific Name	*Andrographis paniculata*
2.	Vernacular Name	Kirta (Sanskrit), Kalmegh (Hindi), Nelaberu (Kannada), Nilavembu (Tamil)
3.	Family	Acanthaceae
4.	Economic part	Whole herb
5.	Active principle/Chemical constituents	Andrographolide (0.8-2%) Stem contains 2%, leaves 2.5%
6.	Distribution	India, Bangladesh, China, Sri Lanka, Thailand
7.	Uses	Antipyretic, Antiinflammatory, Expectorant etc.
8.	Soil and Climate	Well drained sandy loam soils with hot and humid climate
9.	Propagation	Seeds and cuttings
10.	Planting material	Seeds for nursery – 400-500 gms/ha
11.	Spacing	Direct sowing – 15x15 cm Transplanting – 30x 15 cm
12.	Manures fertilizers	25 t FYM/ha along with 75 kg N, 75 kg P_2O_5 and 50 kg K_2O per hectare is required
13.	Irrigation	Mainly grown as a rainy season crop. During long dry periods 2-3 irrigations required
14.	Weeding	First weeding is done after 20-30 days after planting. After this one or two weedings sufficient
15.	Pests and Disease	Hardy plant and not attacked by any serious pest and diseases
16.	Harvesting	Crop ready for the first harvest after 90 to 120 days of sowing when flowering starts

17.	Duration	120 days
18.	Yield/ha	2.5-3.0 tones
19.	Economic / ha	Cost of cultivation – Rs. 15,000 Gross income – Rs. 45, 000 Net profit – Rs. 30, 000
20.	Market	Domestic only
21.	Price	Rs. 15/kg of herb

ASHWAGANDHA

1.	Scientific Name	*Withania somnifera*
2.	Vernacular Name	Ashwagandha (Sanskrit), Asgandh, Punir (Hindi), Kiremallinagida (Kannada), Amukkira Kizhangu (Tamil)
3.	Family	Solanaceae
4.	Economic part	Roots
5.	Active principle/Chemical constituents	Withaferin a and somniferin. Alkaloid content of root is 0.13-0.31%
6.	Species and varieties	*W. congulans* ,Jawahar Asgandh – 20
7.	Distribution	India, North Africa.
8.	Uses	Adaptogenic drug
9.	Soil and Climate	Marginal sandy loam soils, tolerates high pH (upto 8.5). Thrives well in subtropical and semi arid areas with 50-75 cm rainfall
10.	Propagation	Seeds
11.	Planting material	Direct sowing – 5-12 kg ha^{-1} Transplanting – 145 Days old Seedling – 5 kg ha^{-1}
12.	Spacing	20x10 cm
13.	Weeding	Hand weeding at 30 days intervals helps to control the weeds effectively
14.	Pest and disease	The species is tolerant to pest and disease
15.	Harvesting	Harvesting starts from 150-170 days after sowing. The maturity of the crop is judged by drying out of the leaves and

		berries turns to red colour
16.	Duration	180 days
17.	Yield / ha	1200 kg dried roots + 100 kg seeds
18.	Economic /ha	Cost cultivation: Rs. 10, 000 Gross return: Rs. 48, 000 Net profit: Rs. 38, 000 Extra profit from seeds: Rs. 4, 000-10, 000
19.	Market	Domestic and international
20.	Market price	Domestic : Roots – Rs. 40/kg Seeds – Rs. 100/kg International: Roots- $ 22/kg

PERIWINKLE

1.	Scientific Name	*Catheranthus roseus*
2.	Vernacular Name	Madanah (Sanskrit), Sadabahar (Hindi), Smashana kanagale (Kannada), Marukkalankay (Tamil)
3.	Family	Apocyanaceae
4.	Varieties	Nirmal, Dhawal
5.	Distribution	India, Indo-China, Indonesia, Israel, Madagascar, South Africa, USA, Philippines
6.	Economic part	Leaves and roots
7.	Active principle/Chemical constituents	VLB alkaloids like vincristine and vinblastine roots contains 0.75-1.2% leaf 0.6-0.65%
8.	Uses	Leukemia and Hodgekins diseases
9.	Soil and Climate	Wide range of soils and prefers tropical and sub-tropical climate
10.	Propagation	Seeds and cuttings
11.	Planting material	Seeds for direct sowing- 5 kg ha^{-1} Transplanting – 1.5 kg ha^{-1} For seed production – Cuttings For drug purpose – Seeds used
12.	Spacing	45cm x 30cm

13.	Weeding	Requires two weeding in the initial stages of growth. First at 60 DAS and second at 120 DAS
14.	Manures and Fertilizers	FYM @ 10-15 t/ha is applied for obtaining good growth and yield
15.	Pest and disease	Plant is hardy and free from attack of pest and diseases. In some cases little leaf disease occur
16.	Harvesting	Roots of the crop is harvested after 12 months of sowing and leaves can be harvested of 6 months and 9 months after sowing
17.	Duration	10-12 months
18.	Yield / ha	2 tones fresh roots + 4 tones fresh leaves
19.	Economic /ha	Cost cultivation: Rs. 8,800 Gross return: Rs. 32,000 Net profit: Rs. 23,200
20.	Market	Domestic and International
21.	Market price	Domestic market, Roots @ Rs. 12 /kg Leaves @ Rs. 2 /kg

SENNA

1.	Scientific Name	*Cassia angustifolia*
2.	Vernacular Name	Svarana patri (Sanskrit), Sanaysana kapatt (Hindi), Nelavakai (Tamil)
3.	Family	Leguminaceae
4.	Species and Varieties	*Cassia acutifolia, C. obovata, C. italica, C. adovata,* ALFT-2, Sona
5.	Distribution	India, Yemen
6.	Economic part	Pods and leaves
7.	Active principle/Chemical constituents	Sennosides, rhein, aloe-amine Leaves contains : 2-2.5%, Pods: 2.5-3.0%
8.	Uses	Laxative, Purgative and used for habitual constipation

9.	Soil and Climate	Sandy to red sandy loam and prefers warm and dry weather conditions
10.	Propagation	Seeds
11.	Planting material	Seeds 15 kg/ha
12.	Spacing	45cm x 30cm
13.	Weeding	The first weeding cum hoeing is done at 25-30 days and second at 75-80 days after sowing
14.	Manures and Fertilizers	Apply FYM @ 5-10 t/ha
15.	Irrigation	It is economically grown under rainfed conditions. Irrigation given only under prolonged drought conditions
16.	Pest and disease	Leaf eating caterpillars Control: Carbaryl @ 4 g/lit Pod borer control: Spray endosulfan @ 0.05%
17.	Diseases	Damping off Control: Treaf the seeds with thiram or captan @ 2.5 g/kg of seeds For controlling leaf spot disease spraying of 0.15% Dithane M-45 for 3 times in a period of 5-6 weeks
18.	Harvesting	The young senna leaves and pods contain high sennosides First picking of foliage should be done at 50-70 days and second picking is taken at 90-100 days, third picking at 135-150 days after sowing
19.	Duration	180 days
20.	Yield / ha	10 qt of dry leaves + 4 qt of pods
	Economic /ha	Cost of cultivation /ha = Rs. 12, 5000 Gross returns / ha = Rs. 75, 000 Net returns/ha = Rs. 62, 000
21.	Market	Domestic and International

STEVIA

1.	Scientific Name	*Stevia rebaudiana*
2.	Family	Composite
3.	Economic part	Leaves
4.	Active principle	Stevioside (3-10%) and rebaudioside A (1-3%)
5.	Uses	Dietary supplement, Diabeties, Anti-microbial and Anti-fungal
6.	Soil and Climate	Sandy soils with low water table and comes well under sub-humid and subtropical climate
7.	Propagation	Stem cuttings
8.	Planting material	30, 000 plants/acre (6-7 weeks old seedlings)
9.	Spacing	55x25 cm
10.	Irrigation	Requires frequent irrigations
11.	Pest and disease	No pest and disease incidence in this sweet crop. If noticed organic spraying is ideal for it
12.	Harvesting	First harvesting at 4-5 months after planting and subsequent harvest for every 3 months
13.	Duration	Grown economically for 5 to 7 years
14.	Yield / ha	3000-4000 kg dry leaves
15.	Economic /ha	Cost of cultivation Rs. 5, 17, 350 Gross income : Rs. 16, 20, 000 Net profit : Rs. 11, 02, 650
16.	Market	Domestic and International
17.	Market price	Domestic – Rs. 300-400 / kg Planting material – Rs. 15/ seedling

KEEZHANELLI

1.	Scientific Name	*Phyllanthus amarus*
2.	Family	Euphorbiaceae
3.	Economic part	Whole herb

4.	Active principle	Phyllanthin (0.4-0.5%), hypophyllanthin and biflavonoids
5.	Uses	Drug for treating virulent, Hapatitis and Jaundice
6.	Soil and Climate	Prefers red loamy soils (pH 5.5-8.0) and grown in wide range of climatic conditions
7.	Propagation	Seeds (freshly harvested seeds)
8.	Planting material	Seeds for raising nursery 400 g/acre
9.	Spacing	Closer spacing of 15x10 cm
10.	Fertilizers	Application of 50 kg N, 25 kg P and 25 kg K are applied. One ton of vermicompost and 100 kg of neem cake is also recommended
11.	Irrigation	Crop requires adequate irrigation throughout its life period. Irrigation once in a week is required
12.	Weeding	Weed problem in the initial stages should be avoided by taking one or two hand weedings
13.	Plant protection	Except powdery mildew no other serious pest or disease occurs. Control: Sulphur use @ 2 g/lit or spraying of panchakavya @ 15 days intervals
14.	Harvest	The crop ready for harvest in 90 days after planting
15.	Duration	90 days
16.	Yield / ha	Dry herbage – 800 kg; Fresh herbage – 8-10 tonnes
17.	Economic /ha	Cost of cultivation Rs. 6, 000 Gross income: Rs. 16, 000 Net profit: Rs. 10,000
18.	Domestic price	Rs. 20/kg of dry herb

Uses of Important Medicinal Plants

S1. No.	Scientific name/Common Name	Family	Parts used	Active principles	Uses
1.	*Adhatoda zeylanica* Arusha/Malabar nut	Acanthaceae	Leaves, roots, flowers	Vasicine	Expectorant, bronchitis, asthma, fever and jaundice, antispasmodic, anthelmintic, diarrhea, glandular tumours, abortifacient.
2.	*Aloe barbadensis* (Gheekunvar, Ghritakumari, Kumari)	Liliaceae	Leaves	Aleone, Aloesin, Barbulion	Purgative, liver disorders rheumatism, hair growth, chornic ulcer, intestinal worms and cold. The mucilaginous substance obtained from the leaves is commercial product and used as a base material for vanishing cream, moisturizer.
3.	*Alpinia galangal* (Kulanjan: The greater	Zingiberaceae	Whole plant	Methyl cinnamate diterpene	Insecticide. Rhizomes are also used against rheumatism, stomach disorders,

S1. No.	Scientific name/Common Name	Family	Parts used	Active principles	Uses
	Galangal)				bronchial catarrah; as tonic and stimulant.
4.	*Ammi majus* (Honey Plant)	Apiaceae	Fruits	Xanthotoxin, ammoidin	Leucoderma, Stomachic, Carminative and diuretic.
5.	*Andrograhis paniculata* (Kalmegh; Kirayat)	Acanthaceae	Whole herb	Andrographolide, Andrograpin, Paricolin	Antidysentric, antiperiodic, alternative anthelmintic, general debility and dyspepsia, astringent, dysentery, cholera, diabetes, bronchitis, itches and piles
6.	*Bacopa monnieri* (Nirbrahmi: Jalbrahmi)	Scrophulariaceae	Whole herb	Bacosides-A, Bacosides-B	As a brain and nerve tonic, tranquillizer, agaisnt insanity epilepsy and as potent diuretic, cardiotonic, improve intellect, diuretic.
7.	*Calotropis gigantean* (Arka : AK)	Asciepiadaceae	Root, bark, leaves, stalks	Calotropin	Diuretic, purgative. Against intermittent fevers, colds, cough, asthma and indigestion
8.	*Cassia angusitfolia* (Sanae, Bhumiari; Indian Senna)	Caesalpinaceae	Fruits, leaves	Sennosides	Laxative, purgative for habitual constipations
9.	*Catheranthus roseus*	Apocynaceae	Leaves	Reserpine	Antispasmodic, hypotensive, Against

S1. No.	Scientific name/Common Name	Family	Parts used	Active principles	Uses
	(Periwinkle, Sadabahar)		and roots	vinblastine vincristine	leukemia, Hodgkins disease, blood pressure, menorrhagia, sedative, tranquillizing property.
10.	*Centella asiatica* (Mandulkpami; Brahmamanduki)	Hydrocotylaceae	Whole herb	Asiaticoside – A&B	Improving memory, bowel complaints, nervous disorders, female sterility, leprosy
11.	*Coteus forskohlii* Coleus (Pashanbhedi, Patharchur)	Laminaceae	Root tubers	-	Drug for hypertension, congestive heart failures, bronchial asthma, respiratory disorders, painful urination and cancers.
12.	*Chlorophytum borivilianum* (Safed musli, Khiruva, Dholimusli)	Liliaceae	Roots	Saponins	Against gout, rheumatism, abortifacient, tonic and stomachic
13.	*Glycrrhizae glabra* (Madhuka: Mulaithi)	Papilionaceae	Roots	Glycyrrhizin	Tonic, expectorant, demulcent, mild astringent, laxative, against irritation of urinary organs and mucous membrane, preparation of cough syrups. With ghee and honey for cuts and wound
14.	*Gymnema sylvestris* (Gumar: Madhunashini;	Asclepiadaceae	Leaves	Sylvestrin and Gymnemic acid	Blood sugar reducing used against diabetes, cardiach, stimulant, diuretic

S1. No.	Scientific name/Common Name	Family	Parts used	Active principles	Uses
	Merasingi)				
15.	*Mucuna pruriens* (Atamagupta: Kiwachi: Cowhage)	Papillionaceae	Seeds and roots	Lectithin, nicotine, prurieninine, serotonin	Spermatorrhoea, menstrual disorders, nervine tonic, antiparkinsons disease
16.	*Ocium sanctum* (Brinda; Tulsi; Holy basil)	Lamiaceae	Whole herb	Eugenol, Carvocrol	Flavouring food, pharmaceuticals, against sore throat, genitor uriary disorder, respiratory disorders, stimulant diaphoretic, antiperiodic, expectorant, stomachic.
17.	*Phyllanthus amarus* (Jaramla)	-	Whole herb	Phyllanthin.D	Jaundice, eye disease, hiccups, anaemia, leprosy, liver disorders, astringent, stomachic, diuretic, febrifuge, diarrhea, dysentery, colic.
18.	*Piper longum* (Pippali; Indian long pepper)	Piperaceae	Fruits, roots	Piperine	Fruits Alernative, aphrodisiac, against bronchitis, asthma, antidysenteric, leucoderma, jaundice, hiccups. Roots carminative aphrodisiac, diuretic general tonic, joint pain
19.	*Plantago ovata* (Isabgol, Psyllium)	Plantaginaceae	Seed husk	Glucoside, Acubin	Seeds, cooling, demulcent, mildly, astringent, emollient laxative, diuretic. Husks; for constipation, amoebic dysentery and chronic diarrhea,

S1. No.	Scientific name/Common Name	Family	Parts used	Active principles	Uses
					problems of kidney and bladder.
20.	*Rauvolfia serpentine* (Sarpagandha; Serpentina root)	Apocynaceae	Roots	Reserpine serpentine Ajmalicine	Sedative – tensive, antispasmodic, nervous disorders including anxiety states, excitement, maniacal behaviour associated with psychosis, schizolpherina, insanity, insomnia and epilepsy.
21.	*Stevia rebudiana* (Stevia)	Composite	Leaves	Stevioside and Rebudioside	Dietary supplement, healing effect on blemishes, wounds, cuts, used against skin problems like dermatis, seborrhea, reduces elevated blood pressure.
22.	*Withania somnifera* (Ashawagandha)	Solanaceae	Roots	Withanine, Somniferine	Skin diseases, against inflammation, bronchitis, rheumatism, abortion, general toning up of body and as a medicine for impotency in men.

Cultivation Areas of Commercial Medicinal Crops

Common Name	Origin	Cultivated areas	Duration
Safed musli	South India	MP, UP, Tamil Nadu, Kerala, Foot hills of Uttaranchal, HP	8-9 months
Ashwagandha	India	UP, Rajasthan, Hariyana, Punjab	6 months
Senna	Saudi Arabia	Gujarat, MP, Maharashtra, TN, Gujarat, Rajasthan	6 months
Periwinkle	Madagascar	TN, Karnataka, AP, Assam, WB, Orissa	6 months
Aloe	Eastern and North Africa	Rajasthan, AP, Gujarat, TN	5-6 months Perennial (yield upto 5-7 years)
Phyllanthus	America	TN	3 months
Kalmegh	India and Sri Lanka	Assam, Gujarat, Bihar, AP	3-4 months
Glory lily	Tropical Asia and Africa	TN, KA, AP, Orissa, Maharashtra	6-7 monts (Perennial upto 5 years)
Coleus	Tropical Asia and Africa	TN, Gujarat, KA, Maharashtra	5 ½ -6 months
Stevia	Paraguay	Rajasthan	4-5 months (Perennial upto 5 to 7 years)

National Medicinal Plants Board- 32 Prioritised Medicinal Plants

S1. No.	Common Name	Family	Scientific Name
1.	Amla	Euphorbiaceae	*Emblica officinalis* L.
2.	Ashok	Cesalpiniaceae	*Saraca asoka* (Roxb.) de Wilde
3.	Aswagandha	Solanaceae	*Withania somnifera* (L.) Dunal
4.	Atis	Ranunculaceae	*Acontium heterophyllum* Wall. ex. Royle
5.	Bael	Rutaceae	*Aegle marmelos.* L. Corr.
6.	Bumi amala	Euphorbiaceae	*Phyllanthus amarus.*L.
7.	Brahmi	Scrophylariaceae	*Bacopa monnieri* (L.) Pennell
8.	Chandan	Santalacaeae	*Santalum album* L.
9.	Chirata	Gentianaceae	*Swertia chirata* (Roxb. Ex Flem.) Karsten
10.	Daru harida	Berberidaceae	*Berberis aristata*
11.	Giloe	Menispermaceae	*Tinospora cordifolia* (Wild.) Misers ex Hook.f. & Engl.
12.	Gudmar	Asclepiadaceae	*Gymnema sylvestre* (Retz.) R.Br.
13.	Guggal	Burseraceae	*Commiphora wightii/C.mukul* (Hook.ex.stocks) Engl.
14.	Isabgol	Plantaginaceae	*Plantago ovata* Forssk.

S1. No.	Common Name	Family	Scientific Name
15.	Jatamansi	Valerianaceae	*Nardostachys jatamansi* DC.
16.	Kalihari	Liliaceae	*Gloriosa superba* L.
17.	Kalmegh	Acanthaceae	*Andrographis paniculata* (Burm.f.) Nees
18.	Kesar	Iridiaceae	*Crocus sativus* L.
19.	Kokum	Cluciaceae	*Garcinia indica* (Thouars) Choisy
20.	Kuth	Asteraceae	*Saussurea costus* (Fale.) Lipsch./*S. lappa* C.B. Clarke
21.	Kutki	Scrophulariaceae	*Picrorhiza kurroa* Pennell
22.	Makoy/ Manatakali	Solanaceae	*Solanum nigrum* L.
23.	Mulethi/ Liquorice	Fabaceae	*Glycyrrhize glabra* L.
24.	Patharchur	Lamiaceae	*Coleus barbauts* / *C. forskohlii*
25.	Pippali	Piperaceae	*Piper longum* L.
26.	Safed musali	Liliaceae	*Chlorophytum borivilianum*
27.	Sarpagandha	Apocynaceae	*Rauvolfia serpentine* (L.) Benth. Ex Kurz
28.	Senna	Cesalpiniaceae	*Cassia angustifolia* Vahl.
29.	Shatavari	Liliaceae	*Asparagus racemosus* Willd
30.	Tulsi	Lamiaceae	*Ocimum sanctum* L.
31.	Vatsnava	Ranunculaceae	*Aconitum ferox* Wall. ex. Ser.
32.	Viavidang	Myrsinaceae	*Embelia ribes* Burm f.

Distribution of Chlorophytum Species Around the World

S.No.	Species	Other Names	Distribution
1	*C. bowkeri*		
2	*C. heynei*		
3	*C. krookianum*		
4	*C. macrophyllum*		
5	*C. rigidum*		
6	*C. undulatum*		
7	*C. capense*	C. elatum, Asphodelus capensis, Anthericum elatum.	
8	*C. laxum*		Katki Hills, Belgaum, Dharwar, North and South Kanara, Deccan Peninsula in India
9	*C. borivilianum*		Dang forests (Gujarat), Aravali Hills, cultivated species in India
10	*C. arundinaceum*		All districts of Chota Nagpur, Vindhya, Satpura and Aravali Hills, parts of Cental India, Tarai region of N-E Himalayas in Assam, W. Bengal and Bihar. in India
11	*C. tuberosum*	Wild occurence in	

S.No.	Species	Other Names	Distribution
		India	
12	*C. comosum*	C. comosum 'Mandaianum'	Popular garden plant
		C. comosum 'Vittatum' (Spider plant, Aeroplane plant)	
13	*C. zingiberastrum*		
14	*C. bichetii*		
15	*C. malayense*		
16	*C. syngonium*		
17	*C. brasiliense*	Brazilian Chlorophyte	Rare in natural habitat in Brazil
18	*C. amaniense*	Fire Flash	Africa (Gabon and Cameroon)
19	*C. alismifolium*		
20	*C. brevipes*		
21	*C.pussilum*		
22	*C. seretii*		
23	*C. sparsiflorum*		
24	*C. stenopetalum*		
25	*C. parviflorum*		
26	*C. durbanense*		South Africa
27	*C. hasslerianum*		Paraguay
28	*C. virdis*		
29	*C. nepalense*		
30	*C. orchidantheroides*		
31	*C. filipendulum*		
32	*C. silvaticum*		
33	*C. striatum*		
34	*C. baruchae*	*Reported from India*	
35	*C. chinense*		
36	*C. montanum*		

S.No.	Species	Other Names	Distribution
37	*C. madagascariensis*		
38	*C. gallabatense*		
39	*C. zanguebaricum*		
40	*C. piliosissimum*		
41	*C. haygarthii*		
42	*C. attenuatum*		Western Ghats, Southwards to Coimbatore, West Peninsula in India
43	*C. breviscapum*		Parts of Konkan to Travancore in Kerala, Eastern Himalaya, Bihar and West Bengal, Sikkim Himalay, Belgaum and South Peninsula in India